Exploding Into Successful Entrepreneurship

"Bringing Your God-Given Gift To The Surface For Success!"

FINANCIAL EMPOWERMENT WORKBOOK

ANN HANEY

Aaron Publishing
Shelbyville, TN
37160

Published by
Aaron Publishing
Shelbyville, TN 37160
www.aaronpublishing.com

PREFACE

This workbook serves as a companion guide to enhance the teachings in Exploding Into Successful Entrepreneurship. On the following pages you will find life application teachings that provide in depth study and illustrations to help the individual discover how to think outside the box and find success. Many tools will be used to help the student uncover their resources and learn to team them up with their God-given potential to achieve success. The student will be introduced to persuasive writing through sample templates for marketing their product or service in a professional manner.

The first six chapters of this workbook are designed to guide the student from idea to increase. At the end of each chapter the student will find empowerment worksheets to enhance the lessons learned from the preceding chapter. These will allow the student to stretch their thinking to apply the life application principles. In turn this will allow them to develop strategies for success using their gifts. The last chapter is compiled of sample templates of necessary business communication forms. Each template is broken down into components with detailed explanations of each.

It is highly suggested that each student of this program purchase a copy of the book, Exploding Into Successful Entrepreneurship, to use as a foundation for this teaching. Many of the tools used in this workbook are first introduced in the book to help the student lay a solid foundation for business success.

CONTENTS

CHAPTER 1

POSITIONING YOURSELF TO START A BUSINESS

Before anyone starts a business, there is always one thing everyone has in common. What is that one thing we all have in common? Desire to make a change! The desire may not always be derived from the same circumstances, however the same desire has been made to start a new venture. No doubt, you are ready to discover how to start this new venture in your own life with hopes of changing something for the better. You may be unhappy in your current position, financially struggling in your job, or desirous of making a difference in the world we live in.

Whatever the reason one thing is sure—the desires you have can only be accomplished by believing in your ability to do them.

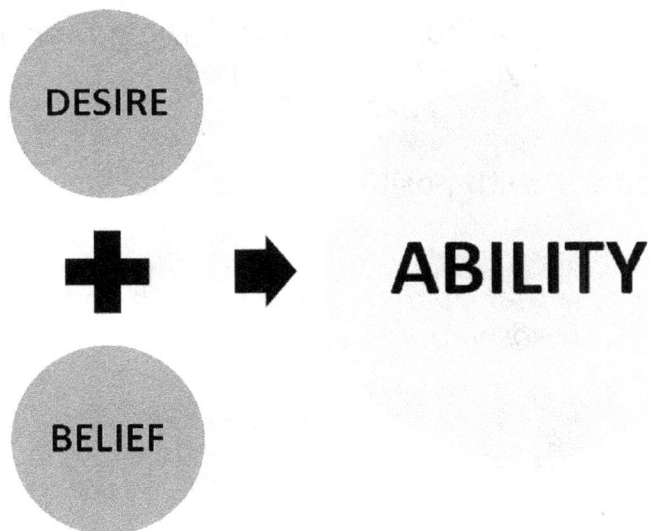

DESIRE

+ **➡** **ABILITY**

BELIEF

The field you choose has many factors we will look into in this workbook However, there are 5 basic requirements to position yourself for any field of success. These could be summed up in one statement—"The condition of your mind determines the outcome of your position." Once your mind is trained to think positively your actions will soon follow. Let's look at these 5 key principles.

1. Know who you are—(open mind for realizing you have a gift)

"Thou art highly favored, the Lord is with thee…."
Luke 1:28

2. Cast out fear—(controlled mind for defeating opposition)

"But, the angel assured her, 'Mary you have nothing to fear…"
Luke 1:30

3. Identify your gift—(learning mind to obtain knowledge)

"God has a surprise for you…And Mary said, 'How can this be?'"
Luke 1:31,34

4. Remain spiritually empowered—(trusting mind for direction)

"The Holy Spirit will come upon you, the power of the Highest hover over you."
Luke 1:35

5. Surround yourself with positive people—(seeking mind to find supporters)

"And did you know that your cousin Elizabeth conceived a son, old as she is?…. Nothing you see, is impossible with God."
Luke 1:36

Know who you are	Cast Out Fear
Identify Your Gift	Remain Spiritually Empowered
Surround Yourself With Positive People	

Understanding you have a call on your life to fulfill is your very first step. Once you have made this decision don't be surprised when fear grips you. Anytime we venture out in a new direction we will be faced with some form of anxiety. Fear may attack you in questioning, availability of resources, other people, etc... Some false beliefs that may come against you are:

You're not experienced enough!

Your too old!

No one will buy your product or service!

Your too young!

You won't make enough to support your family!

You don't have enough money!

After defeating the opposition identify areas in your life you are gifted at. Think about what you would like to do with your life. What are your dreams or vision for the future? It is important after you determine your vision that you do not box in how this vision will come about. Let me explain. My desire was to become a teacher. My vision caused me to think "Public School Teacher" as my only way of completing my desire. I felt a leading to home school my children, thus a different type of teacher. Now, after 15+ years of teaching my children, I now teach men, women and teens on various empowerment topics.

Moving toward your goal will require you to remain empowered mentally. How do you do this? Stay in prayer and daily devotion to remain positive as you venture toward entrepreneurship. There will be times when it seems hope is all you have with no prosperity in sight. But, it is through this continual hope that happenings occur. If the hope dies, so does the happening. When you become discouraged, pray harder.

"I do believe, help my unbelief."
Mark 9:24

Finally, surround yourself with positive people. Usually, one of the first things that happens when you become excited about your vision is your desire to share it with other people. Be careful who you share your vision with and how you let their response affect your actions. Many times the excitement you feel is not immediately recognized by others. Do not become discouraged when it seems you are the only one excited. Don't lose your excitement! Continue to pursue your dream. As you commit to this pursuit your excitement will become contagious. A contagious vision causes others to get on board with your dream and want to take part in what you are doing. When you can build this type of excitement, you are building clientele, sponsors, and cheerleaders for your business. Word of mouth continues to be the number one way to build and maintain a successful business.

While you are on your way to building excitement, connect yourself with other business minded individuals. One way to do this is by joining local community business networks. These are numerous and should be easy to find. Simply use a search engine to locate business associations/groups. Most will allow you to attend once or twice for free then will require a yearly fee to remain a member. Try several and decide which ones produce the most potential for your type of business and join these. Do not feel intimidated because you are just getting started. Dress for success, walk with success, talk with success! Your attitude about who you are and what you do will empower you to do it and cause others to believe you are already doing it. This is not to behave deceptively, but rather confidently, confident in your ability to accomplish what you have set out to do.

Business contacts are important, but friends who have conquered the challenges you are facing or are going through the same challenges can be a great source of encouragement. These are your accountability partners. Take their advice, heed their warnings and be strengthened by their faith.

There will be times when doubt comes in, but the goal is to drive it out. Don't let it stay too long, work as though success is already at hand and you will find your doubt turn to a refreshing and new ideas waiting to be enacted.

Finally, when nothing is happening continue on with the last project you started. Sometimes a new idea only surfaces when an old one is completed.

EMPOWERMENT WORKSHEET A

My Positive Characteristics:

_____ex. Creative_____

_____

_____

_____

_____

Challenge Areas:

_____ex. shy_____

_____

_____

_____

_____

Fears About Starting A Business:

_____ex. Lack of mathematical skill_____

_____

_____

_____

Overcoming Those Fears:

_____ex. Counsel with an accountant_____

_____

_____

_____

_____

Your gift: Alternative Ideas for Using Gift:

ex. Teaching _____   _ex. Public Speaking_ _____

_____   _____

_____   _____

_____   _____

_____   _____

Daily Mental Empowerment:

ex. Devotions _____

_____

_____

_____

_____

Network of Business Believers:

ex. Friends, acquaintances

_____   _____

_____   _____

_____   _____

_____   _____

_____   _____

My Vision: _____

_____

CHAPTER 2

DISCOVERING YOUR FIELD OF OPPORTUNITY

All businesses generally derive from one of 4 different elements or a combination of elements.

BUSINESS FIELD PYRAMID

NEED

FRUSTRATION

HOBBY

TALENT

Look back at your vision from page 12. Does your vision come from one of the 4 elements on the pyramid? Chances are that it does. In order to discover our field of success it must stem from something we are passionate about and enjoy doing. After all isn't it your desire to enjoy your job while making a living? This is what makes entrepreneurship so appealing. Too many people spend their lives in jobs they hate just to keep food on the table and pay the bills. Isn't it time to reverse this cycle by discovering your passion for prosperity.

Let's look at each of these in more detail:

1. A NEED— A need will be anything that you have found necessary in your life that is not readily available. You have encountered a situation where a tool, service, or product would have made your situation easier. You must remember you are not the only one like yourself. There are many people just like you who would benefit from the very thing you are needing yourself. Here's an example:

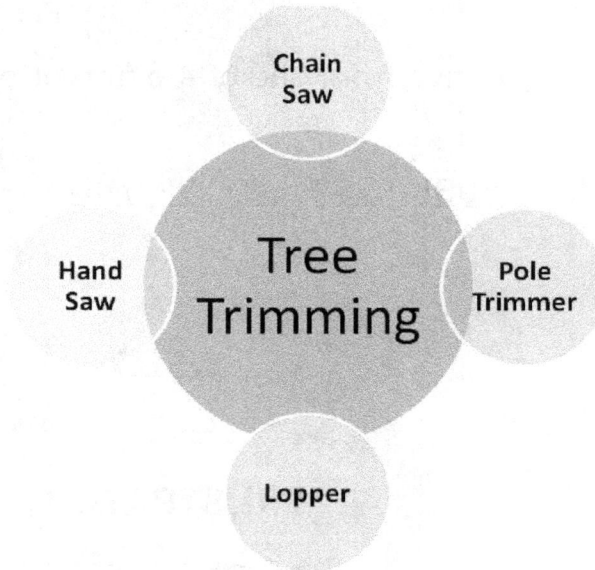

Chain Saw

Hand Saw

Tree Trimming

Pole Trimmer

Lopper

2. A FRUSTRATION— A frustration will be anything that drives you absolutely crazy if it is not done or done to your satisfaction. It might not bother someone else, but there are many who just like yourself can't stand to see it undone. Here's an example:

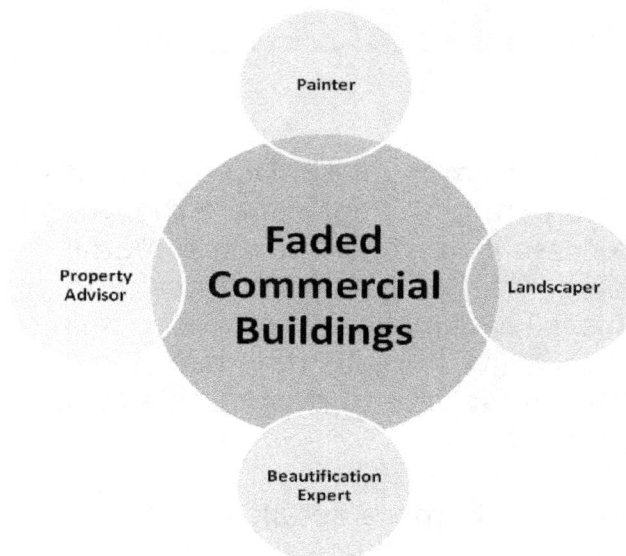

Painter

Property Advisor

Faded Commercial Buildings

Landscaper

Beautification Expert

3. A HOBBY— A hobby is what you spend your free time doing for relaxation. After completing the daily duties your extra time finds you engaging in this activity or method of relaxation. Your hobby can become your career. Here's an example:

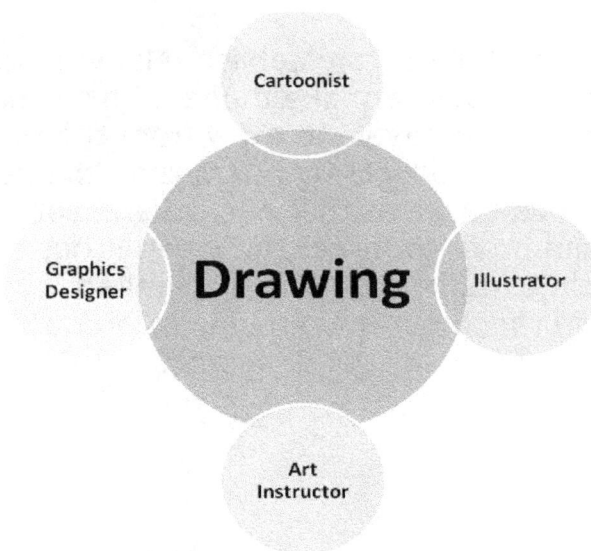

Cartoonist

Graphics Designer

Drawing

Illustrator

Art Instructor

4. A TALENT— A talent is something people tell you you're good at. Your talents may be numerous and often can combine to grow into many careers. Be willing to branch out into as many directions as you can when using your talents. They have an ability to add to the significance of each other and multiply your income when used together. Here's an example:

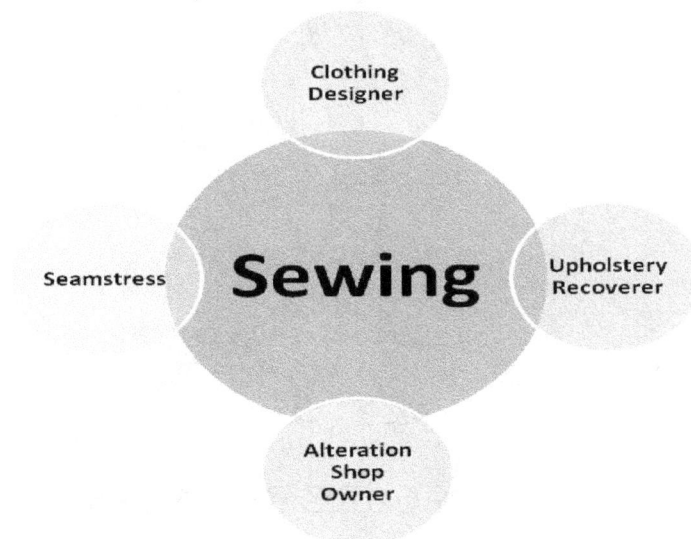

Clothing Designer

Seamstress

Sewing

Upholstery Recoverer

Alteration Shop Owner

You have probably noticed that your gift area should not be boxed in with limited thinking. From these examples you should be able to see that careers can range from simple ideas to more complex ideas. Simple ideas produce as much potential as complex ideas. Think about transportation—most people own bicycles and cars. As a matter of fact a typical household probably has more bicycles than cars. Whatever you do, don't think your idea is too simple to make a big impact on your future.

All ideas take time and effort to establish. Many make the mistake of thinking they must have money to make money. This is not true. Start where you are at with what you have and grow from there. Reinvest your profits into growing improved products by purchasing the necessary tools to do so. A stable business is a business that has several sources of income. Think about a tree. It can produce more fruit when it has several branches, but with only 2 branches the fruit potential is limited. Look at the example below to see how to branch out a main idea to produce income from different sources. This allows for year round income.

CHRISTMAS LIGHT HANGING

GARDEN TILLING

TREE TRIMMING

GUTTER CLEANING

LEAF REMOVAL

LAND-SCAPING

SNOW REMOVAL

LAWN CARE BUSINESS

EMPOWERMENT WORKSHEET B

NEEDS—

List items or services you always find yourself needing that you don't own or can't find anywhere:

_____

_____

_____

_____

TALENTS—

List something others say you are good at or something others are always asking you to do because they know you do a good job:

_____

_____

_____

_____

HOBBIES—

List things you do in your free time that provide relaxation or refreshing to your life after a hard day's work:

_____

_____

_____

_____

FRUSTRATION—

List something that stresses you or causes you a desire to fix or correct:

_____

_____

_____

_____

Look back over your list and write down from easiest to hardest 8 of the previous items you could produce or do. This will give you an idea of what things might be within your reach presently. Do not disregard the others; work your way to developing several fields of income.

_____

_____

_____

_____

_____

_____

_____

YOUR BRANCHING BUSINESS

_____

(List Your Top Idea Here)

In the boxes below list ways you can expand the income of this business through other services and/or products. Be creative!

CHAPTER 3

WEEDING THE FIELD FOR PROFIT

We have discussed the circumstances surrounding mentalities for success in chapter 1. However, it is important to be aware that starting a business is not an easy road to success. Success will be accomplished when one realizes the things that try and keep the business from reaching it's desired goals.

Think about what occurs before a field is planted. It is prepared through plowing to make the soil acceptable to receive the seed. However, herbicide is generally applied prior to seed planting to kill weeds that can overtake a planted crop. What does this mean in regards to your business? It is important to weed your business of any hindrances to it's growth. It is interesting to note that weeds can coexist with newly planted seeds for a period of about 3 weeks until the root systems of the seeds began to spread out at which time they are hindered by the weed that has been allowed to remain.[1] In other words, if you do not identify the hindrance to your business early on, its affects will surface to hinder you down the road. Many farmers prepare their field through herbicides in the fall to prepare for the spring planting.[2] Preparation for business directly affects the size of the crop you will produce!

It is very important to discover how these hindrances occur and tear them down at the root. In order to do this you must discover what causes these hindrances and stop the spread of them. This is the only way for a business to survive and thrive. Let's take a look at some hindrances to a healthy business:

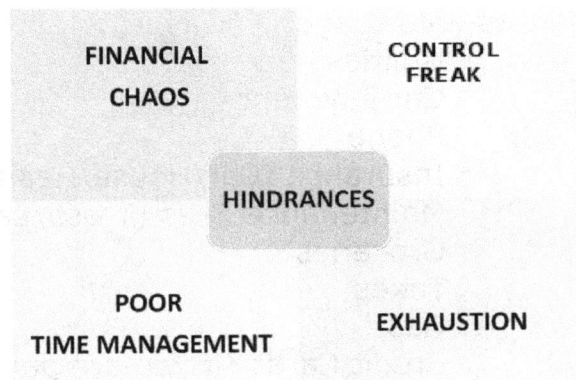

FINANCIAL CHAOS   CONTROL FREAK

HINDRANCES

POOR TIME MANAGEMENT   EXHAUSTION

[1] farmprogress.com
[2] wikipedia.org/wiki/weed_control

Each of the previous hindrances will grow discouragement and discouragement eventually overtakes your vision of success. What are some solutions to weeding out these hindrances that can allow for the spread of profit? Let's take a look and see:

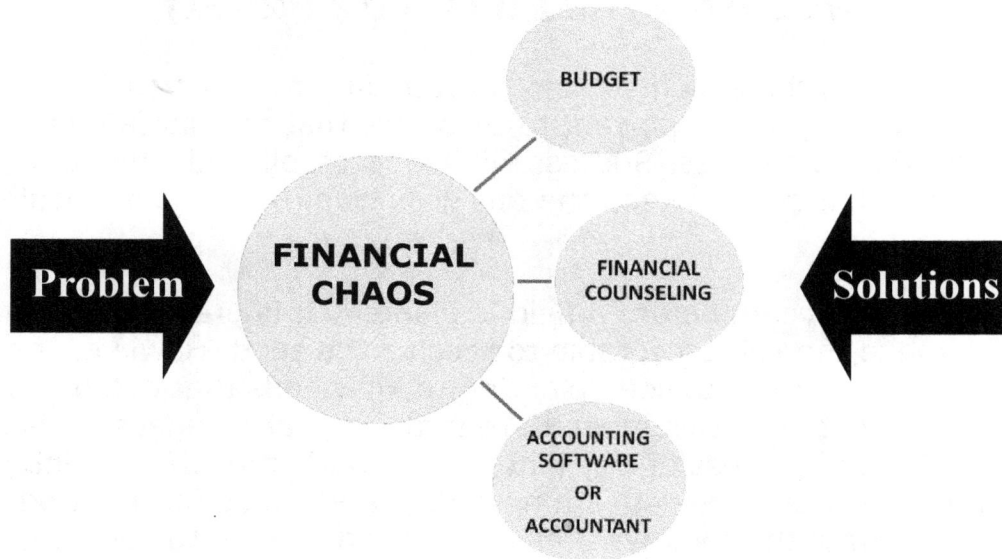

1. PREPARING A PERSONAL BUDGET—

Every household needs a budget and so does every business. Without this planning money can easily disappear leaving you wondering where it went. **Always remember a poorly run household will carry over into a poorly run business**. A budget is basically a financial plan that helps you to determine income and expense. It is a crucial part to financial planning. Many of the items will not refer to the entrepreneur, however will affect the employee becoming the entrepreneur. A personal budget should consist of several components:

Monthly Expenses—Mortgage
Utilities
Car Payment
Phone
Insurance (Car/House/Health)
Maintenance Fees (Trash/Lawn Care, etc..)
Groceries
Taxes
Gas
Credit Cards (if you are paying any off)
Charitable Donations

Miscellaneous Expenses— Savings
       Emergency Fund (appliances, car repairs,
        etc.)
       Clothing
       Entertainment (vacations, eating out, etc.)
       Miscellaneous (gifts, holidays, hair cuts,
        pets, etc...)
       Investments
       Retirement
       Education (college, classes, school, etc.)

Income— Job (take home pay)
   Social Security
   Disability
   Side Income (self employment this will be what you pay
    yourself from your business and will also appear in your
    Business Budget)
   Interest
   Dividends (a bonus received by shareholders)
   Bonuses (from job)
   Child Support
   Retirement (IRA's or 401 K)

PREPARING A BUSINESS BUDGET—

Once the individual has established the components of the personal budget they are ready to start thinking about a business budget. Many of the components of this budget will need to be adjusted as the entrepreneur progresses and discovers the exact income of the business. However, it is necessary to make a plan before the money starts rolling in so the business does not spend more than it takes in. (Many will be similar to that of a personal budget.) A business budget should consist of these components:

Monthly Expenses—Mortgage (Rent or Owned Building if applicable)
       Utilities
       Phone
(If work from home   Insurance (Worker's Comp, liability, equipment,
contact an accountant   etc...)
to determine how to   Equipment Expense (repairs, etc..
apply these expenses)   Labor (employees)
       Taxes
       Charitable Donations
       Gas

Marketing (banners, ads, media, radio, etc..)
Inventory (product creation)
Office (supplies, business cards, letterhead, etc..)
Food (business luncheons, etc..)
Internet (hosting fees, web design, etc..)
Travel (hotels, plane tickets, etc..)
Income—Sales
Sponsorship

It will be necessary to adjust your budget (either personal or business) as a pattern of income can be tracked. Generally, it will take a year or so to learn the up and down seasons of a business. Most businesses will be fairly well-grounded after 2 years. As the owner you should project your income in three areas as to not overspend during this time period. In other words have a projected low, medium and high for your sales. Always believe you will achieve the high, but be prepared for times of low sales. This will mean not spending all of your income from one job or sale to restock supplies, not leaving yourself income to make the hosting fee to keep your website online.

FINANCIAL COUNSELING—

You don't need to know everything to start a business. Knowledge is gained by tapping into the resources around you. Many of the resources can be found in what others have already discovered. Ask for advice from those who are successful in their business. Ask a friend who is an accountant or schedule a meeting with an accountant to learn how to set up your business to achieve the greatest success.

"Without consultation, plans are frustrated, but with many counselors they succeed." Proverbs 15:22

ACCOUNTING SOFTWARE OR ACCOUNTANT—

It will be necessary to track all income and expenses for your business. There are software programs that can make this process easier for you, like Quickbooks. There are classes offered on using these programs. One great resource is youtube.com, where you can watch how-to videos that will answer a lot of questions you may have. However, keeping ledgers of income and expenses the old fashioned way may be more comfortable for you. If neither of these give you the peace of mind in running your own business it will be necessary to hire an accountant. However, you will need to keep all your income and expense receipts together for them to do an efficient job. The better your records the less it will cost you at the accountant.

Another hindrance we often see in business is poor time management. Time management is not only important to the success of a business, but to the success in life.

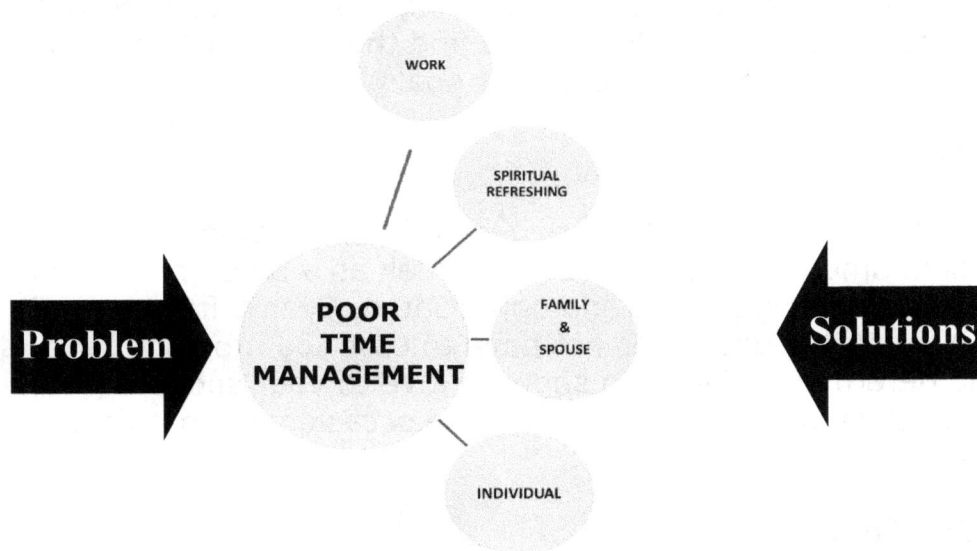

WORK

SPIRITUAL
REFRESHING

Problem → POOR
TIME
MANAGEMENT

FAMILY
&
SPOUSE

← **Solutions**

INDIVIDUAL

MANAGING WORK—

If you are just starting your business you will find the time involvement to be more excessive, especially if you have another job as well. It is important however, that you set aside a specific amount of time for business start up daily. Do this by making a check list of items to accomplish. Work on this list daily trying to complete one item a day. One thing you do not want to do is allow your time involvement for work to tap into the other three solution areas above. Leave work at work and pick up where you left off the day before. A business is not built overnight. Excessive work does not get a job done quicker, it produces mental strain and numerous errors which in turn have to be corrected.

SPIRITUAL REFRESHING—

A day that starts with Godly wisdom will be led by Godly wisdom. Spend time each morning in devotions to prepare yourself for the situations of the day that will arise. This is your equipping and without it you will find yourself handling things in less productive ways. God is the beginning of wisdom and your day needs to start with wisdom to express wisdom all day long. This will multiply your time without correcting unnecessary mistakes.

FAMILY TIME—

Family time is time to laugh, play, watch a movie together, have dinner to-gether, or hugs and home movies. These are the rewards of hard work. Money cannot replace these and time cannot recreate these moments. If they do not become a part of every day your life and the lives of those you love will suffer. Getting where you are going must be accomplished with the ones God has placed in your life. If you find the family a hindrance to your goals, then it is time to reevaluate your goals.

SPOUSE TIME—

Date night delivers refreshed marriages and builds communication gaps. Setting aside time for your spouse each week as a token of love, not obliga-tion, will keep marriages alive and appreciated. Even if it's a drive in the country. A profitable date does not have to cost you money. Money should not be the determining factor in showing love to your spouse. (Although, it is important to show special tokens of love occasionally that do cost you something.)

INDIVIDUAL TIME—

We were each created with desires, characteristics and personalities with tendencies for certain pleasures. If we do not take time to nurture these tendencies we will lose our identities. Hard work must be rewarded with something that provides the individual with a refreshing. Anything from go-ing to an auction, rummage sale, getting your nails done, a bubble bath to reading a book. Take time to make time for yourself!

The problem of overworking may still be in control of your life, even with the past suggestions. Here is a way to combat the mindset of "if I don't do it myself, it won't be done right."

Problem → **CONTROL FREAK** — DELEGATE DUTIES / MAKE A TO DO LIST / HIRE WORKERS ← **Solutions**

DELEGATE DUTIES—

Entrepreneurs have the perfect opportunity to develop a mentorship education for their children. By allowing and delegating your children to take part in the business you have chosen you are laying the ground work for their future success. Do not think it cruel to have them help you work the family business? Think of it as doing them a great injustice if you don't expect it. Only through doing does one become equipped to succeed in life. Watching is not enough to prove one's ability. If the family benefits from the business, the family should be involved in helping the business succeed. This means letting go of some of your control and teaching them to lead.

TO DO LISTS—

Take the necessary time to write down a list of things that need to be accomplished, assigning tasks for all family members. A good boss has a vision and plan for tasks to accomplish the vision. Check off the items as they are accomplished and continue adding to the bottom of the list to keep production moving forward. Never do half of one job and half of another. Discouragement will set in as the list seems to grow without the benefit of marking anything off. Lists only work when tasks are completed one at a time. Too many ideas and not enough accomplishments will never meet success.

HIRE WORKERS—

As your business grows it will become necessary to hire workers. Remember to pay reasonable wages for the job at hand. Pay what you would expect to be paid if you were hired to do the work. Start small by hiring only enough workers to help with the increased work load without depleting the profits. If you can't make a profit your employees will soon suffer with lay offs.

Finally, for the last hindrance. This list is not exhaustive by any means. It is important to identify other things that might try and keep you from your goals and discover solutions for them as they occur. If you focus on your short term and long term vision you should be able to quickly identify things that may negatively affect the success of that vision.

Don't discourage when the road looks like it is unending or even when it looks like many side roads are tempting your direction. Distractions and discouragements are not a hindrance unless you allow them to control your actions. Remain the course and you will arrive at your destination.

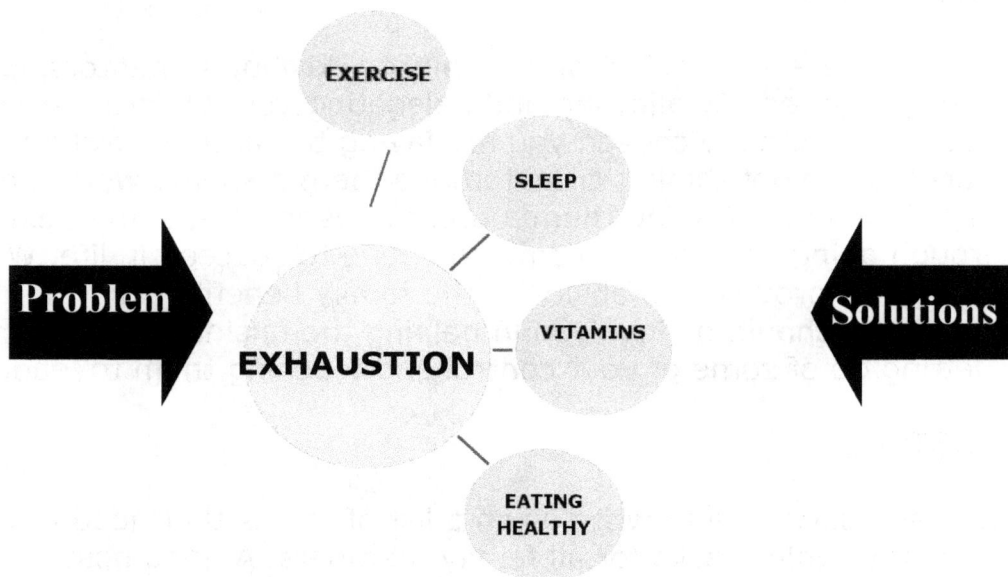

```
                    EXERCISE

                              SLEEP


     Problem ▶              VITAMINS        ◀ Solutions
              EXHAUSTION


                         EATING
                         HEALTHY
```

SLEEP—

Most people will stretch themselves to the limit when it comes to sleep. Just a few more hours of work or play surely won't hurt or will it? Eventually, it does catch up with you and hinders future progress. How much sleep do I really need you may wonder. Here is what the National Sleep Foundation recommends.[1]

How Much Sleep Do You Really Need?	
Age	Sleep Needs
Newborns (0-2 months)	12-18 hours
Infants (3 to 11 months)	14 to 15 hours
Toddlers (1-3 years)	12 to 14 hours
Preschoolers (3-5 years)	11 to 13 hours
School-age children (5-10 years)	10 to 11 hours
Teens (10-17)	8.5-9.25 hours
Adults	7-9 hours

Source: National Sleep Foundation

The problem with not getting enough rest on a regular basis is that eventually you will have to catch up. If sleep wasn't important God wouldn't have created it. A good balance of sleep will keep your mind alert and an alert mind makes for wise business decisions.

VITAMINS—

[1]http://www.sleepfoundation.org/article/how-sleep-works/how-much-sleep-do-we-really-need

The body must have a balance of adequate vitamins and minerals to function at its best. Most of this can be accomplished through a proper balanced diet. However, with busy schedules most people do not get the needed daily vitamins they need from all the food groups. This can be supplemented by taking a daily multivitamin along with other vitamins to enhance your body's function. For example, suffering from tiredness and mental strain can be alleviated by taking B12.[1] Here is a website that will help you determine what vitamins you need to take to achieve overall health— www.healthsupplementsnutritionalguide.com. Do remember that vitamins are not a replacement for good eating habits and proper sleep.

EATING HEALTHY—

Now for a balanced diet, the most challenging area for all people. Our lives are busy and with fast food so readily available, good nutrition is often sacrificed. You have heard the saying, "You are what you eat." So the question is what do you eat? Is what you put in your body providing you the energy and longevity of life you hope for? After all, once you have built a successful business don't you desire to be healthy enough to enjoy the benefits of it. We see it all the time-people who spend their whole life building their business while they are actually tearing down their bodies on the way. If you don't eat enough to keep your energy up, how do you expect to accomplish the tasks required to fulfill your vision.

EXERCISE—

Yes, our least favorite word is really necessary. Even if it means just walking, it is crucial to your overall health. The Dept. of Health and Human Services recommends at least 150 minutes of Aerobic Activity a week. This can be brisk walking, mowing the lawn, etc... In other words a person can spend 2 1/2 hours a week in these type of activities to help stay healthy. This can be spread out over the course of the week. They also recommend strength training twice a week. Strength training could be weights, hoeing a gardening, tilling, anything that exerts strength to accomplish.[1] Mayo Clinic tells us there are 7 main benefits that are derived from exercise. Exercise controls weight, combats health conditions and diseases, improves mood, boosts energy, promotes better sleep, improves intimacy, and can be fun.[2] I am a firm believer in these and do this on a regular basis with my children. Yes, I attest to the fact that with exercise your overall abilities to improve your life in all areas are directly related to exercise. Take the time to stay in shape and the other things in your life won't need more of your time to fix.

[1]http://www.mayoclinic.com/health/exercise/AN01713
[2]http://www.mayoclinic.com/health/exercise/HQ01676

PERSONAL BUDGET

INCOME:

INCOME:	P	A
JOB		
SOCIAL SECURITY		
DISABILITY		
SIDE INCOME		
INTEREST		
DIVIDENDS		
BONUSES		
CHILD SUPPORT		
RETIREMENT		

EXPENSES:

EXPENSES:	P	A
MORTGAGE		
UTILITIES		
CAR PAYMENT		
INSURANCE-CAR		
INSURANCE-HOUSE		
INSURANCE-HEALTH		
TRASH		
LAWN CARE		
GROCERIES		
TAXES		
GAS		
CREDIT CARDS		
CHARITABLE DON.		
CABLE		
PHONE		
MISCELLANEOUS		
SAVINGS		
RETIREMENT		
INVESTMENTS		
ENTERTAINMENT		
EMERGENCY FUND		
CLOTHING		
EDUCATION		

PROJECTED INCOME

ACTUAL INCOME

PROJECTED EXPENSES

ACTUAL EXPENSES

30

BUSINESS BUDGET

INCOME:

	P	A
SALES		
SPONSORSHIP		

EXPENSES:

	P	A
MORTGAGE		
UTILITIES		
WORKER'S COMP		
INS. LIABILITY		
INS. EQUIPMENT		
INS.-HEALTH		
TRASH		
LAWN CARE		
EQUIPMENT		
TAXES		
GAS		
LABOR		
CHARITABLE DON.		
MARKETING		
PHONE		
MISCELLANEOUS		
OFFICE		
FOOD		
TRAVEL		
INTERNET		
INVENTORY		

PROJECTED INCOME

ACTUAL INCOME

PROJECTED EXPENSES

ACTUAL EXPENSES

31

TIME MANAGEMENT
CHART

Week 1--List all the activities you do in the correct time box. Do this for 1 week and see how you spend your time.

Week 2—Change your activities to be more productive and get more done than last week.

	WK 1	WK 2		WK 1	WK 2
6:00 AM			2:30 PM		
6:30 AM			3:00 PM		
7:00 AM			3:30 PM		
7:30 AM			4:00 PM		
8:00 AM			4:30 PM		
8:30 AM			5:00 PM		
9:00 AM			5:30 PM		
9:30 AM			6:00 PM		
10:00 AM			6:30 PM		
10:30 AM			7:00 PM		
11:00 AM			7:30 PM		
11:30 AM			8:00 PM		
12:00 PM			8:30 PM		
12:30 PM			9:00 PM		
1:00 PM			9:30 PM		
1:30 PM			10:00 PM		
2:00 PM			10:30PM		

EMPOWERMENT
WORKSHEET
F

TO DO TEMPLATE

TO DO LIST

Priority	Activity	X

MONDAY
TUESDAY
WEDNESDAY
THURSDAY
FRIDAY
SATURDAY
SUNDAY

EMPLOYEE TEMPLATE

This template serves as a guideline to list the extra tasks associated with your business which can be delegated to family members or potential employees.

JOB TITLE	JOB DESCRIPTION	PROSPECTS

34

CHAPTER 4

Considering Your Business

You probably have some ideas by now to help you find a starting point in establishing your own career. The key question that comes to most people's mind at this point is "How do I get started?" This is a very legitimate question. The good news is, there is an answer! You are at the point that requires consideration on behalf of the top idea you have for increasing profit. There are two key factors that need to be considered before you jump right in. Let's look at them in detail:

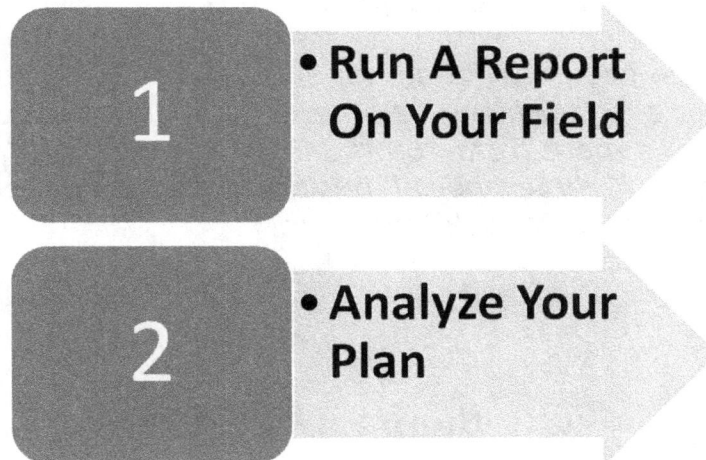

1 • Run A Report On Your Field

2 • Analyze Your Plan

RUNNING A REPORT ON YOUR FIELD—-

This requires 4 key components to uncover before you can determine the potential profitability of a business.

Growth Potential

Growth Potential requires you to determine if your idea has the possibility of branching into increasing profits. It is important to determine the success potential of a business idea before sinking all your efforts and funds into it. Keep in mind if you are operating in your gift, success is assured, but there are ways to achieve that success through your gift. Growth Potential is determined by an ideas ability to create rising profit and full time employment. Ask yourself a few questions regarding your idea:

1. Is my idea seasonal?

2. Is my idea gender specific?

3. Is my idea geographically specific?

4. Is my idea cost effective?

(In other words does it cost more to make than I can profit from it?)

5. If a service, does my idea require more time at less hourly rate than an average job in today's job market?

(If the answer is yes, the benefits do not surpass working as an employee. The idea is to make a better living as an entrepreneur than as an employee. If your business takes more from you than it gives to you, it needs to be reconsidered. However, remember all business startups generally require a little more work. You need to look long term.)

Demand

Now it's time to determine the demand for your product or service. The importance of this is crucial. The demand is directly related to your potential clients. After all, if no one buys it or uses it, it will not produce the success you hope for and you won't be in business long. So how do you determine the demand for your product? Use the following resources to discover this:

1. Check the want ads in local paper, national papers, and internet

(This will help you discover if people are asking for your service or product)

2. Keep on top of news stories that prompt a reoccurring need

(For instance, if burglaries are commonly occurring this might produce a need for an affordable home security system or neighborhood watch service of some kind. Obviously there is a problem in need of a solution)

3. Be alert to businesses like yours that have to schedule out services weeks in advance or have to back order products to fill orders.

(This is an indication that they have more business than they can keep up with. This could be due to staffing problems or time management problems, however this is an open door to opportunity that exists for your business.)

Competition

Competition needs to be considered, but don't let it discourage you from pursuing what you believe to be the career opportunity for you. Chances are there will be others who have a gift similar to yours or even the same. However, if it is your gift it was meant to produce success in your life. God does not equip you with a gift for failure.

*"Make a careful exploration of who you are
and the work you have been given, and
then sink yourself into that.."*
Galatians 6:4

Discover your competition in the following areas:

1. Internet
2. Local Competitors
3. National Competitors
4. Mail Order Competitors
5. Home Based Competitors

What should you ask yourself regarding your competitors:

1. How long have they been in business?

2. How large is their cliental?

(This can often be determined by their size, their parking lot-full or empty, their number of employees, etc..)

3. What is the location of the business?

(This will help you determine where to open your business. You probably don't want to open your business on the same block as your competitor.)

Past Success Or Failures

It is often beneficial to research the successfulness of past services or products. Determine why a product was or was not successful. This will give you insight on what needs to be improved and what works well. There is no need to reinvent the wheel. This works in business as well. Learn from others mistakes and successes. Here is a list of questions you should consider:

1. What failures in this field have occurred in the past?

2. What went wrong in these businesses or products?

(Was it a lack of money management, a malfunction with the product, etc..)

3. What have successful businesses done that contribute to their continuance?

(Was it excellent customer service, timely deliveries, quality products, etc...)

Analyzing Your Plan—-

Analyzing your idea for a business is an important factor. Basically, analyzing means to consider in detail. It only makes sense to determine what your business is going to require in order to be sure you are up for job.

Here are some components you want to consider before you start up your business:

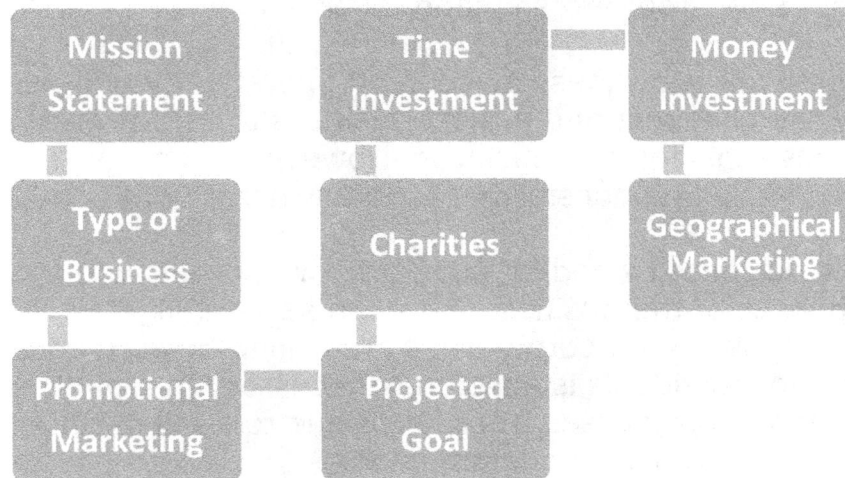

Mission Statement	Time Investment	Money Investment
Type of Business	Charities	Geographical Marketing
Promotional Marketing	Projected Goal	

MISSION STATEMENT—

This should be why you do what you do. In the early part of this chapter we looked into discovering our competitors. A good question to ask yourself when making your mission statement is this, "What do I hope to offer that my competitors do not?" Let's look at an example:

"John Doe Graphics is committed to providing equal and exceptional service to all clients with the purpose of providing complete, convenient, and quality service."

This tells your customers you do not show favoritism, you will be thorough in your services and you will go out of the way to convenience them.

Your mission statement does not always have to be something different that is offered. The importance is to let the customers know you care and your heart in why you do what you do. Here's another example:

"Ann Haney Ministries is committed to reaching individuals and families who find themselves victims of a challenged economy by teaching them how to be abundant survivors."

TYPE OF BUSINESS—

Determine if you plan on running your business as a Sole Proprietorship or a Partnership. Either way it will be important to have a Board of Directors who advise you in making wise business decisions. Let's look at the difference between a Sole Proprietorship and a Partnership.

Sole Proprietorship— A business owned and operated by one person
It is generally the cheapest and easiest business to establish. Most start up companies choose this form of business. However, in this type of business the owner assumes all responsibility of the business, both good and bad.

Partnership—A business owned by generally two parties who share the income and expenses of the business. This can serve to lighten the work load of each individual assuming both parties are willing to work equally. A contract between the individuals is absolutely necessary in a partnership. Many would-be-successful businesses have failed due to a fall out between the partners. (Generally over misunderstandings.)

PROMOTIONAL MARKETING—

What marketing will your business be doing to promote its services or product? There are numerous ways to market a business today, some detailed others quite simple. It will be necessary to determine what types of marketing you plan on using for the business start up because this will affect the cost of the start up. See chapter 6 for more on marketing strategies.

TIME INVESTMENT—

All businesses require an investment of time. However, when a business is initially started your time may be somewhat limited if you are presently in a career. Make a wise evaluation of the time the business you are considering will require of you upon start up. If you don't have time to invest in your business idea it might be necessary to start on a smaller scale and build up to it. Remember this doesn't mean you won't accomplish it, but that it will progress in stages. If your idea is bigger than the time you have, you can easily become discouraged and never reach your goal. Remember the branches, which branch do you need to grow first.

CHARITIES—

It will be necessary to determine what charities you have a heart to support with part of your income. All successful businesses understand that a portion of their proceeds must be given out if they are going to prosper.

PROJECTED GOAL—

What is your goal for your business? Is your desire to bring home both spouses from the work force? Is your desire to prepare a well established business for your children's future? Do you wish to have 10 published books within the next 5 years? Whatever the goal, it will be necessary to make long term as well as short term goals. Long term goals are necessary to keep you moving forward, however short term goals will keep you from becoming discouraged.

MONEY INVESTMENT—

Most businesses will require some type of financial investment. However, you have heard me say, "You don't have to have money to make money." So what does this mean exactly? In the beginning stages it will be necessary to do what you can with what you have. If you have heard my testimony on my first published product, you remember I produced my first idea on my computer printer. My next group (of 10 copies) were produced in an Office Print Store. Eventually I moved up to a table top copier, then a large commercial copier. Finally, much of my product is professionally printed although we still reproduce much of our products in house. This product which started small gradually become a 5 year running best seller. In the beginning there were no profits, however stages of commitment grew into money in hand. Use what you have, where you're at and consistently progress and your idea will become a reality. As far as the money investment determine what portion of your income could be set aside weekly to invest in your business.

GEOGRAPHICAL MARKETING—

Does your idea have the potential to produce income in the area in which you live or will it be necessary to offer it in region specific areas? For example, if you have recorded a country music CD you would probably want to look for opportunities in the Nashville, TN area. If you are designing a new type of cleaner for snow skis, you would obviously want to market this to places that receive sizeable amounts of snow each year. The more versatile your product is the more sizable the income potential. That doesn't mean you shouldn't try other things, but start wisely and know your geographical potential.

EMPOWERMENT WORKSHEET H

What is the growth potential of my product?

_____ Seasonal

_____ Geographical Specific

_____ Gender Specific

_____ Cost Effective

Where have I seen a demand for my product/service?

Businesses _____

Websites _____

States _____

People _____

Who are the top competitors in my field of business?

In my town_____

Online _____

Past successes of others in my field of business?

_____

What made others fail in my field of business?

_____

What solution can I offer to lessen my chances for failure?

_____

_____

Write a mission statement for your business

_____

_____

_____

Sole Proprietorship Or Partnership? _____

How do I plan on promoting my business in the beginning stages:

_____   _____

_____   _____

How much time do I have to devote to developing my business?

_____ daily   _____ weekly

What charities do I wish to support:

_____   _____

How much money will I need to create my first product or offer my service?

_____

What are my short term goals: What are my long term goals:

_____   _____

_____   _____

_____   _____

_____   _____

_____   _____

CHAPTER 5

Starting Your Business

Up to this point we have been considering the aspects surrounding our business idea. Now you are ready to take the proper steps to get your business off the ground. The importance of laying the ground work can not be underestimated. A well built foundation has the ability to reach greater heights. Let's look at some key components to the startup of a business.

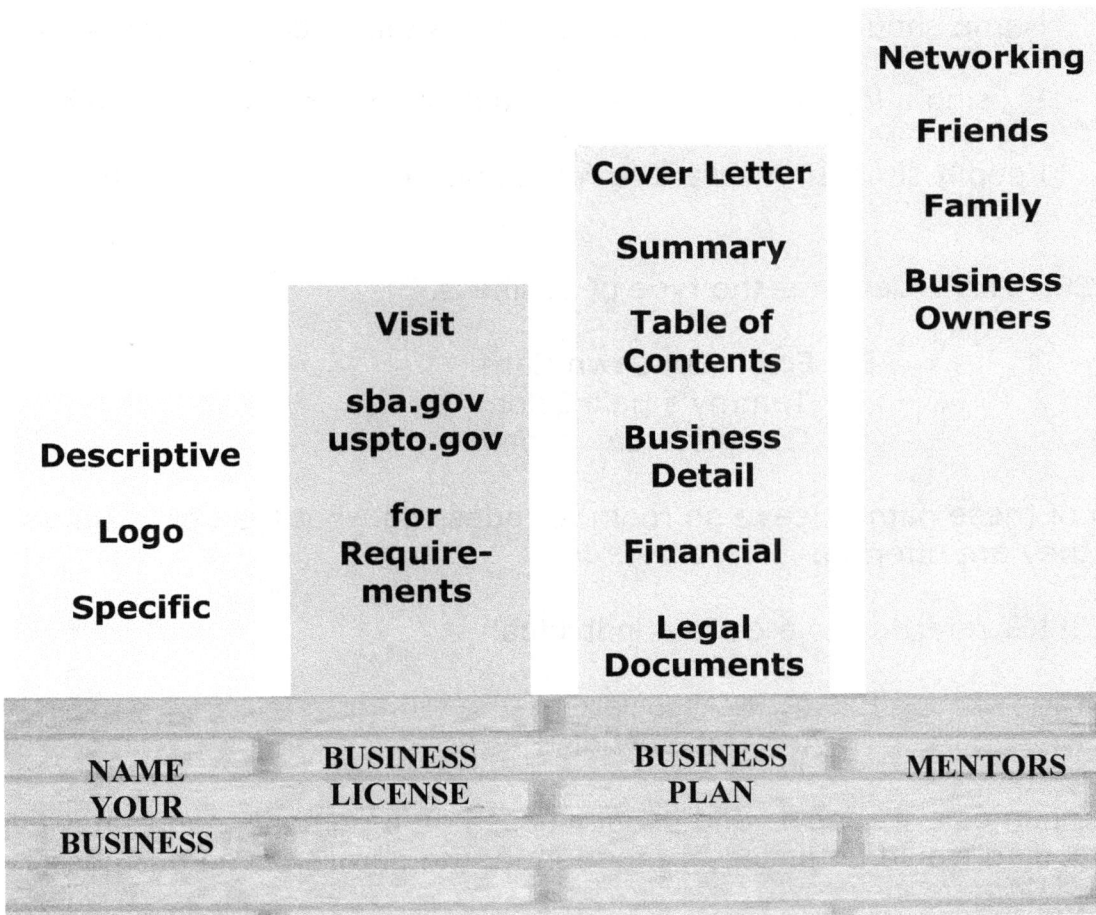

			Networking
			Friends
		Cover Letter	Family
		Summary	Business Owners
	Visit	Table of Contents	
	sba.gov uspto.gov		
Descriptive		Business Detail	
Logo	for Require-ments	Financial	
Specific		Legal Documents	
NAME YOUR BUSINESS	**BUSINESS LICENSE**	**BUSINESS PLAN**	**MENTORS**

BUSINESS NAME—

What's in a name? A name has the potential to increase your business if chosen carefully. A name needs to clearly identify the service or products a business offers. If a potential customer is left guessing what your business does, then chances are they will go somewhere else. Here are some bullet points to help you decide wisely.

*Name should be legible

*Name should identify service or product (if you choose to go with abbreviations or your name, have a subheading that gives the client an idea of what you are offering.)

Ex...Ann Haney Ministries-Helping You Unlock An Abundant Life
In this we see that the ministry is based on helping others build abundance.

*Name should not be so close to others that it causes confusion

*If using a logo in the name it should not overpower the name itself

*Keep it short (if it's hard to remember you will lose potential clients)

DESCRIPTIVE: identifies the type of business.

Ex. Fresh Cut Lawn Care
Tammy's Hair Salon
Complete Car Repair

Each of these names leave no room for guessing what type of business service they are offering.

SPECIFIC: referring to a certain individual

Ex. JRI & Associates
Ann Haney Ministries

These names are specific and usually based on a person's name, however a subheading would be necessary to identify the nature of the business.

Ex. JRI & Associates
"Counseling With Care"

46

LOGO: can serve to detail the nature of the business, however it must be kept simple. The importance should be placed upon the name and the logo weaved into it. There are many types of logos. A graphics designer can help you create a unique logo that will enhance your business and catch the eye of your client while maintaining the significance on your business name. Visit hqdesignservices.webs.com for some unique ideas at competitive prices.

OBTAINING A BUSINESS LICENSE—

Go to sba.gov for detailed information on obtaining a business license. It will be necessary to have a business license to operate your business and can be obtained from the county in which you will be operating from. On this website you will find the necessary information needed to obtain a tax id number, register your business and receive any licenses or permits to operate your business. Depending on the type of business you will be operating the requirements differ.

BUSINESS PLAN—

Business plans serve as a guideline for starting and running a successful business. There are many components that need to be included in a well written business plan. Let's break these down:

COVER LETTER COMPONENTS:

>   *Name of Business
>   *Slogan
>   *Logo
>   *Copyright w/Company Name
>   *Date & Revision if applicable
>   *Contact Information (Name, Address, Phone, Email)

**See templates in chapter 7 for a sample of a Business Plan Cover Letter.

TABLE OF CONTENTS:

    This will be a quick overview of what will be included in the following pages. See www.bplans.com for other samples to fit your style of business.

(The following is a sample table of contents and should be adjusted to meet the needs of your business.)

Ex. I. Summary
    A. Mission
    B. Vision
  II. Business Detail
    A. Services/Products Offered
    B. Marketing
      1. Strategies
      2. Potential
      3. Target
    C. Competition Analysis
    D. Operations
      1. Distribution
      2. Pricing
      3. Product Development
    E. Employees
    F. Board of Directors
    G. Insurance (Property, Liability, Health, etc.)
  III. Financial
    A. Sales Potential
    B. Loans
    C. Equipment & Supplies
    D. Profit Loss Statements (all transactions in a business)
    E. Long Term Analysis (3 year plan)
    F. Cash Flow (money spent & money received)
  IV. Legal Documents
    A. Tax Returns
    B. Lease Agreements
    C. Supplier Contracts
    D. Licenses

MENTORS—

A mentor is a trusted guide or counselor (career coach.) Starting a business brings with it many questions. It is a good idea to have several people serve as your mentors to efficiently run your business. Many areas will affect the efficiency of your business. Financial, Emotional, Physical, and Spiritual. Trusted family members and friends who have your best interest in mind can keep you encouraged. Business owners who you admire or have shown a pattern of success will serve as great teachers. They will be able to help you understand the ups and downs that come with running a business and will have possible solutions to handling business conflicts they have seen in their own businesses. Remember before you can be a good teacher yourself, you must be willing to learn from others. This brings us to networking.

Find organizations in your area by searching online or ask other entrepreneurs about groups within the area. These are usually abundant and most will allow you attend the first meeting free, however most will have a yearly fee if you decide to join. My suggestion would be to attend several and see which ones your business is a good fit for.

The power of networking is crucial to all successful businesses. If networking poses a fear to you remember that the things you fear have been feared at some point by everyone. No one starts out with all the answers and if they think they do they are misleading themselves as well. Let me encourage you to connect with small business groups, county business organizations, other entrepreneurs and anyone you can learn from. Be yourself when you attend these meetings. A good communicator is always a real person not a person pretending to be perfect. None of us are perfect. However, we must believe in the value we possess and walk and talk with confidence. Believe in what you're doing and believe in your ability to do it.

PRICING—

Pricing your product or service does not have to be scary. Do your research and see what your competitors are charging. Consider your cost and look for the most cost effective way to produce what you offer. Don't overbuy; work with what you have where you are at. A general rule of thumb is this—

<u>Selling to Retailers</u>
Retailers—Generally want a 40-50% discount off suggested retail
Suggested Retail = The price you want the item sold for

Ex. Your cost—$3
    Retailers Cost—$9
    Suggested Retail—$15

Obviously when you sell direct you will make a greater profit. However, selling to retailers allows more visibility of your product and can increase the number of products sold. One word of advice is this—don't show favoritism in business dealings. Believe in what you have and don't under sale yourself out of fear. If you don't believe in what you offer, how do you expect others to?

EMPOWERMENT WORKSHEET I

LIST THE NAMES YOU ARE CONSIDERING FOR YOUR BUSINESS:

_____   _____

_____   _____

_____   _____

LOGO IDEAS YOU ARE CONSIDERING:

_____

_____

_____

_____

_____

_____

SKETCH YOUR LOGO IDEAS BELOW:

LIST FAMILY AND FRIENDS WHO WOULD SERVE AS A TRUSTED MENTOR:

_____   _____

_____   _____

_____   _____

LIST BUSINESS OWNERS WHO YOU COULD CONTACT FOR MENTORSHIP:

_____   _____

_____   _____

_____   _____

LIST CAREER COACHES WHO COULD HELP GUIDE YOU IN BUSINESS STARTUP:

_____   _____

LIST COUNTY OR SMALL BUSINESS ORGANIZATIONS WHOSE NETWORK YOU COULD ATTEND MEETINGS AT:

_____   _____

_____   _____

_____   _____

_____   _____

WRITE A BUSINESS PLAN FOR YOUR BUSINESS ON ANOTHER SHEET OF PAPER FOLLOWING THE GUIDELINE ON PAGE 48.

CHAPTER 6

Growing Your Business

The foundation should now be laid to begin the building the project upward. There are 4 main components which will help you achieve business growth. How well you incorporate these within your business will have a great impact on your business growth in regard to speed and success. These all serve as an important piece to building the perfect picture of your business.

INVESTING—

Let's look at the actual definition of what it means to "invest." To invest in something means to furnish with power, give qualities and abilities to.

It should be your goal to look for ways to empower your business by giving it qualities and abilities that grow success. We looked at one way of investing in chapter 2 when we talked about "Branching Out Your Business." This can serve as a way to produce multiple cash flow from several related components. However, investing in your business can also come from other areas not related. Investing can be time, money, talents, bartering with others who can offer your business something. I want to take a look at one particular area we have not looked at yet, "bartering with others." Bartering is an exchange of goods or services without involving money. How can this help your business? Simply this—we can't do it all, but together we can all do it! Chances are you have something that can benefit someone else and they have something that can benefit you. You have heard me say before, "you don't have to have money to make money," so what do others have that can make you money in exchange for something they need?

Ex. Facts—-John Doe starts a new web design business
John Doe has no potential clients

Facts—-Jane Doe has a large network of business associates
Jane Doe's website needs updated

Investment—John Doe can offer his services to Jane Doe in exchange for some recommendations and introductions

Ex. Facts—-John Doe wants to start his own business & needs a a mentor

Facts—- Jane Doe has written a book and needs a good review

Investment—-Jane Doe mentors John Doe and he gives her the review she is needing

Do you get the idea? There is no end to what can be accomplished when we learn to invest in our business by helping one another meet their goals. Some investments only require thinking outside of the box. When you hear the word "investment" stop thinking only money.

Working together is growing together. Both parties should benefit the business of one another.

GRANTS—

Grants can serve as another way to raise money for your business. Many companies give away grant money within certain guidelines. It will often be based upon how the money will be used, type of business, etc… Many non-profit companies give away grant money as well. There are many online resources to finding these grants, however sba.gov would be a good place to start as they are aware of most of the grants available to businesses.

MARKETING—

This is probably one of the best ways to grow your business exposure and the possibilities are limitless. Everyday we are seeing more and more marketing strategies appear. I want to give you a list of some of the best sources available currently:

Blogging	Radio	Press Releases
Microblogging	Sponsorship	Video
Media	Website	Vendor Fairs/ Expos
Product Submission	Test Marketing	Article Distribution
Social Networks		

And More......

BLOGGING— A shared online journal posting about personal experience, product or services.

Comments may be posted here to help gain word of mouth promotion of your business. Some web builder programs allow you to use a blog within your website. However, one popular blog site is wordpress.com and another is blogger.com, where you can easily begin your own blog site to talk about your product or services. Encourage friends, family, business associates to leave positive comments and even ask questions that would allow you to expand upon what you offer. Starting a discussion starts a chain reaction to discovering needs and offering solutions by marketing your product/ services.

MICROBLOGGING—A blog site that limits the number of characters which can be posted.

This is a great way to gain creditability. It is ideal for quotes, links to websites or product reviews, etc...Twitter is among the most popular microblogging site.

MEDIA— Television coverage for your business. One way to maximize on this possibility is by planning a community event. Offering an incentive to the community can bring publicity to your business giving you the opportunity to expand.

PRODUCT SUBMISSION— Submitting a product to retailers.

This should be done in several areas: online, local businesses, large retailers, etc.. Don't be afraid to promote to the large as well as the small. God will not allow you to get in over your head. You will want to include several things when you submit your product:

> *Sample of Product (These generally will not be returned)
> *Business Card (Logo, Name, Slogan, Address, Website, Email)
> *Product Submittal Letter (Cover Letter)
> *Dealer Terms & Conditions (Pricing, Shipping, Return Policy, Handling of Backorders, Tax Exempt # request, etc...)
> *Tri-fold Brochure giving an overview of your product (include bullet points of product/service highlights, what it can do for their company, what it will do for the customer, statistics, testimonies of users, availability date, etc..)

It is usually best to place these items in a nice business portfolio folder. These are relatively cheap and can be purchased at any office store.

SOCIAL NETWORKS—Sites that connect you and your business with the world.

This one is a big plus to the marketing world. Here you will connect with friends, family, business associates, school mates, etc.. Keep people updated with what you offer, what you are doing, where they can find your events, and learn all about your business and you.

Some of the well-known sites are Facebook, My Space, Schoolfeed, Branchout, and LinkedIn. The first three are more personal sites to keep connected, whereas the last two are more business minded. Joining several sites gives you more visibility. LinkedIn is especially helpful as it allows you to join groups specific to your business or interest and start a conversation with others. This allows you some control in steering towards your business advantages.

RADIO COVERAGE—Any coverage on the radio is coverage to add to your portfolio for creditability.

Most broadcast talk shows have a podcast (a playback of media files for the computer or mobile device). These can usually be linked directly from the radio website to your website for more visibility. Link your interview on your website. Depending on your business, most radio shows do PSA's (Public Service Announcements) monthly which are required to remain on the air. Contact them to see if your event, might fall in line with their regulations for this type of coverage.

SPONSORSHIP— A supporter or advocate of a business or person.

Sponsors usually back a business or person in exchange for promoting their business. This backing can come in many forms. Often sponsors will pay a fee to a business to promote them. Other sponsorships might be guarantees to your business (usually in the form of money) in exchange for email lists, etc... I do not believe it is good business practice to give, sell or exchange your customers information unless they have given their approval to exchange this information with the sponsor. Some sponsors will do giveaways in exchange for the customers contact information but only if they agree to it.

WEBSITE—The best tool for marketing what you do.

Every business must have a website to compete in today's market. There are many options for websites. You can create it yourself or use web designers. The advantage to having a web designer is their knowledge on keeping your site up-to-date, attractive, and they make changes as you need them for a monthly hosting fee. Check out classAmedia.com for professional web building options at reasonable rates.

TEST MARKETING—Trying out your product/service for success.

Family, friends, neighbors, etc... are great places to start your test marketing. Allow them to use your product or service for free in exchange for advice on ways to improve and testimonials on the success they have experienced in their own lives from using your product or service.

PRESS RELEASES—An announcement formatted for a news release on your new product, workshop, or service.

These are very beneficial and should be written from a reporters view point. Link these to Facebook, Twitter, LinkedIn, etc...There are several press release sites, however, PRLOG.com is a great free site to start with.

VIDEO—Visual marketing tool that delivers excellent product/service coverage.

Youtube.com has become the number one site for posting short videos to promote business services, products, as well as events, how-to's, etc... Maximize upon this to open a world of visibility for what you do. A simple home video can be shot and uploaded to youtube. However, videographers can do amazing transitions to a video by adding teaser trailers, backdrops, music, and text to provide a professional touch to your business. ClassAmedia.com offers great services in this area with an extensive and impressive portfolio of experience.

VENDOR FAIRS & EXPOS—Events for displaying your product or demonstrating your service to a large number of people in one area.

Many fairs/expos offer workshops and featured speakers. It is always best to try and access this opportunity as it promotes fan buy after your presentation. Search for specific events pertaining to your product/service. These are readily available. Most will have a booth rental fee and can vary based on the size of the event.

ARTICLE DISTRIBUTION— A way to promote what you do through magazines or online resources.

Squidoo is one resource for creating a web page promoting your business.

Submit articles to magazines specific to your type of business. Your article should passionately describe why you do what you do and why you believe in it. Remember the more excited you become about your business or product the more excitement you will build. You must cause people to catch your vision in order to grow your business. If people don't get motivated they don't get moving. What can you do to motivate your audience?

*Be persuasive
*Be truthful
*Be confident
*Stick to your subject
*Be concise

CUSTOMER SERVICE—Building relationship with your clients through quality service.

This is the stability in your business. A happy customer is a returning customer. A returning customer brings others with them. Always do your best to keep your customers happy. Without them your business will fail. It is likely you will have customer challenges from time to time that are beyond your control, however it should be your number one desire to try and remedy an unpleasant business deal in any way you can as long as it does not cause you to change your morals. Don't fret about the few that just can't be satisfied after all your attempts. Chances are if they won't work with you, their reputation precedes them with others as well. Do your best and leave the rest to God. Post a customer service guarantee at your business and include it with your product and on marketing material.

EVENTBRITE—A site for posting your event where people can sign up and get tickets to it.

This site allows you to promote your event and link it to your other online social sites. It is a great way to track the projected attendance and help you prepare for an exceptional event.

There are many forms of marketing available. These are suggestions, but full details of each of these sites should be obtained from their website to determine forms of marketing that meet your business criteria.

EMPOWERMENT WORKSHEET J

LIST AREAS OF YOUR BUSINESS WHERE YOU NEED HELP:

_____

_____

_____

_____

WHAT SERVICES CAN YOU OFFER OTHERS:

_____

_____

_____

_____

WHAT BUSINESSES/PEOPLE COULD YOU OFFER YOUR SERVICES TO IN EX-CHANGE FOR WHAT YOU NEED:

_____

_____

_____

_____

LIST POSSIBLE GRANTS YOUR BUSINESS MIGHT QUALIFY FOR:

_____   _____

_____   _____

DESIGN AND ORDER BUSINESS CARDS FOR YOUR BUSINESS.

LIST THE COMPONENTS THAT ALL BUSINESS CARDS SHOULD HAVE:

      *
      *
      *
      *
      *
      *

WRITE A PRODUCT SUBMITTAL LETTER

PREPARE A TERMS & CONDITIONS SHEET FOR YOUR PRODUCT

DESIGN A BROCHURE OR FLYER FOR YOUR SERVICE/BUSINESS USING A TEMPLATE ONLINE (Microsoft Publisher has many tools that help with these type of projects.)

SET UP SOCIAL MEDIA MARKETING IF YOU HAVE NOT DONE SO ALREADY.

LIST POSSIBLE SPONSORS TO CONTACT FOR YOUR BUSINESS:

_____

_____

_____

_____

START A BLOG TO PROMOTE YOUR PRODUCT/SERVICE

LIST THE COMPONENTS YOU NEED IN A WEBSITE:
(Ex, shopping cart, products page, mission statement, etc...)

_____   _____

_____   _____

_____   _____

WRITE A PRESS RELEASE ANNOUNCING YOUR PRODUCT/SERVICE

WRITE AN ARTICLE FOR SQUIDOO

LIST POTENTIAL VENDOR FAIRS OR EXPOS YOU COULD ATTEND WITH YOUR PRODUCT/SERVICE:

_____

_____

_____

_____

LIST PEOPLE YOU CAN TEST MARKET YOUR PRODUCT/SERVICE TO:

_____   _____

_____   _____

_____   _____

WRITE A SCRIPT FOR A VIDEO PRODUCTION PROMOTING YOUR BUSINESS SERVICE/PRODUCT:

WRITE A CUSTOMER SERVICE GUARANTEE FOR YOUR BUSINESS

***Use the Sample Templates in the next chapter as a guideline for completing these projects.

CHAPTER 7

Sample Business Templates

*Sales Letters
*Cover Letters
*Product/Service Quote
*Detailed Proposal
*Terms & Conditions
*Consignment Contract
*Facilitator Form
*Email List
*Attendee Survey Sheet
*Business Cards
*Charitable Donation Log
*Copyright Page
*Press Release
*Free Lance Writing Contract
*Video Script
*PSA Announcement
*Brochures
*Flyers
*Business Plan

SAMPLE SALES LETTER COMPONENTS

PURPOSE— To introduce potential customers to your product or service and give them enough information to entice them to desire your services/products. It will be the first thing the potential customer will see and is important to make it clear and concise. Submittal Portfolios should include this sales letter, sample of product, business card, press release (optional), brochure and terms and condition sheet.

Part 1—Business Logo

Part 2—Your Name
      Position
      Address
      Phone Number

Part 3—Date

Part 4—Greeting (Use the person's contact name, usually this will be the head of the buyers department. If you do not know it use "Dear Reviewer."

Part 5—Introduction of product. How this product will entice potential buyers. Use statistics whenever possible (but do not overuse them.)

Part 6—Tell the retailer how this product can help their business personally. Let them know how they can learn more about this product through enclosed brochures, flyers, etc…

Part 7—Thank them for previous business by reminding them of a product they carry of yours that has done well. (If this is your first product submittal this step will be omitted, however, if not this will serve to remind them of their past success in dealing with your business.)

Part 8—Offer your availability to answer any questions or comments they might have regarding your product. Be sure and include your direct email.

Part 9—Your closing should offer your enthusiasm and confidence in working with the customer.

Part 10—Signature

Part 11—Name
      Title

SAMPLE SALES LETTER

1

{

Sue Smith
 CEO
Adams Publishing
000 San Dino Dr.
Tulepo, MS 32169
233-697-4560

March 19, 2012

Dear Retailer,

We would like to introduce you to another great product by Adams Publishing. The title of the book is "Exploding Into Successful Entrepreneurship-Bringing Your God-Given Gift To The Surface For Success." This is a Biblical based teaching on discovering, applying and succeeding with individualized gifts. We believe this book will inspire and equip future entrepreneurs. The average American is finding their cost of living in 2012 exceeding their wages, resorting to both parents working, often 2 jobs just to make ends meet. The federal minimum wage stands at $7.25, however 5 states are below minimum wage and 4 states have no minimum wage requirement. Thus, the reasoning people are seeking answers for success.

Please take time to review this product, as we believe it has the ability to reach your marketing area and increase your sales potential. Please see the enclosed brochure, sample product and dealer term sheet for details.

We appreciate your continued business with the Homeschool Daily Planners for Curriculum, Unit Studies, and High School.

If you have any questions regarding this item, please feel free to call, write or email us at the following: sue@adamsprinting.com

We look forward to a continued working relationship with you.

Sincerely yours,

Your Signature Here

Sue Smith
 CEO

SAMPLE COVER LETTER COMPONENTS

PURPOSE—— **To introduce yourself for a potential position with an organization or business. This can be for a speaker position for an upcoming event or future engagements.**

Part 1—Business Logo

Part 2—Address
　　　　Phone Number
　　　　Email

Part 3—Contact
　　　　　Position
　　　　Company
　　　　Address

Part 4—Date

Part 5—Greeting (Use the person's contact name)

Part 6—What can you offer to the organization that causes them to view you as an asset to their business?

Part 7—What past experience makes you a benefit to their company?

Part 8—What are others saying about you that would help the company to see your creditability with others?

Part 9—Identify how you would like to be of service to their business, organization or company.

Part 10—Closing with signature

SAMPLE COVER LETTER

000 Thomas Blvd
San Diego, CA
219-883-4716
sue@ahm.com

John Doe
Event Planner
SCI Foundation
912 Bart Ln
Baltimore, MD 58413

January 11, 2012

Dear John Doe,

Do you desire to help others learn how to make money in a challenged economy? Ann Haney Ministries is committed to helping people unlock abundant futures by teaching them how to use their God-given skills to create cash flow. I am a highly motivated, entertaining speaker who makes it my goal to see all people achieve success by turning the victim mentality into an overcomer's mentality.

I have had extensive experience in many areas including, but not limited to:

*Hundreds of past speaking engagements to small and large groups
* Humble personality that communicates well with all crowds
*Published Author of 18 products
*CEO of Aaron Publishing and Founder of Ann Haney Ministries
*Columnist for the Nashville Examiner
*Extensive media and radio coverage for life changing techniques

Here's what past attendees are saying:

"Ann relates all principles taught to real life application that I can understand." Terri M., Springfield TN
"I feel equipped to conquer whatever challenges I face after hearing Ann speak on the power of the overcomer."
Mike S., Chicago, IL

"Ann's honest humility shows forth through her willingness to share her life through personal examples of trials and triumph that I can relate to." Tonya P., Hopkinsville, Ky

I would love the opportunity to serve your organization at your Middle TN Expo on March 18, 2012.

Best regards,

"YOUR SIGNATURE HERE"

Sue Smith

SAMPLE SERVICE/PRODUCT QUOTE COMPONENTS

PURPOSE-— To provide potential customers with a detailed quote for your services or products you will be delivering to them.

Part 1—Business Logo, Name of Business, Address, Phone Number

Part 2—Website and Email

Part 3—Date of Proposal
Title of Product Or Service You Will Be Delivering
Name of Customer
Address of Customer & Phone Number They Can Be Reached At
Starting Date (date the work will begin)
Delivery Date (completion date of work if being delivered)
Customer Pickup Date (date customer can pick up if desired)

Part 4—Objectives or Services (These are the bullet points for listing the details regarding what services or products you will be completing for the customer.)

Part 5—This is where you can list options for the customer to mark their preference. If the objectives have already clearly been identified as to what will be completed, here you will put the total cost of the product/services offered.

Part 6—In this part you will list the payment requirements for your business. These may vary, ex. Half down, remainder at delivery of product or completion of service, net 30 days, due upon receipt, due at start of job. These really depend upon the nature of your business and your overhead.

Part 7—A disclosure statement will tell customers what they can expect from you. This can also be described as the "Customer Satisfaction Guarantee."

Part 8—Customer's signature and date of approval. The approval date should be the job beginning date unless other arrangements have been made with the customer.

Part 9—Be sure and put a statement regarding the maturity of this quote. Quotes should never be open ended. Doing so can create loss of income as materials fluctuate in cost.

SAMPLE PRODUCT/SERVICE QUOTE

ANN HANEY MINISTRIES
ANN HANEY, FOUNDER
000 Template Dr., Sample, MN 38941
PHONE: 000-000-0000

Website: www.annhaney.com   Email:me@myownboss.com

DATE OF APPLICATION/PROPOSAL:_____

TITLE OF PROJECT OR SERVICE:_____

BEGINNING DATE: _____

EXPECTED DATE OF COMPLETION:_____

APPLICANT/CLIENT: _____ TITLE: _____

ADDRESS: _____ PHONE: _____

_____

<u>OBJECTIVES OR SERVICES:</u>

*2 hour power point presentation

*Workbook/Study Guide for each attendee

*30 day online counseling via email

*Copy of instructional CD

QUOTE FOR ABOVE OBJECTIVES OR SERVICES: _____

**This quote reflects labor and expenses for the above objectives/services.

PAYMENT: Half down when the job is accepted and the remaining balance due on the day services/ objectives are completed. Cash, Check or Credit Card payable to Ann Haney Ministries.

DISCLOSURE: It is the desire of Ann Haney Ministries to efficiently and professionally complete the objectives/ services above to meet the needs of the above mentioned applicant/client. Ann Haney Ministries will provide open communication to the applicant/client regarding any questions/comments regarding this proposal.

_____   _____

(Applicant's Acceptance Signature)   (Date of Acceptance)

Above Quote Will Be Valid For 30 Days

SAMPLE DETAILED PROPOSAL COMPONENTS

PURPOSE—— To provide potential customers with a detailed quote for your services or products you will be delivering to them.

Part 1—Business Logo, Name of Business, Owner/Position, Address, Phone Number, Website and Email

Part 2—Purpose of your offered service

Part 3—Your personal biography of past and present achievements.

Part 4—Objectives or Services (These are the bullet points for listing the details regarding what services or products you will be completing for the customer.) Here you will want to give detail of what you will be talking about or providing in an clear outline for easy reading.

Part 5—This is where you can list the requirements you have for bringing this product or service to the potential customer.

Part 6—This will tell when you will be able to deliver the above products/services and instructions on how.

Part 7—A recap of your contact information including your email, phone and website.

Part 8—Anything else you need to tell your potential client about your business. Ex. Nonprofit, All Sales Final, Money Back Guarantee, etc...

ANN HANEY MINISTRIES
ANN HANEY, FOUNDER
000 BLANK LANE, SAMPLE, TN, 37160
PHONE: 000-000-0000

Website: www.annhaney.com   **Email:me@myownboss.com**

FINANCIAL EMPOWERMENT PRESENTATIONS

PURPOSE:

It is the goal of these presentations to enhance the lives of all individuals through life application teachings in a motivational hands on approach with time allotment for questions and answers. Ann's goal is helping people uncover their resources and team them up with their God-given potential to achieve success.

BIO OF ANN HANEY:

Ann Haney has been an entrepreneur since 2001. She is the CEO of Aaron Publishing and the founder of Ann Haney Ministries. Ann is an author and publisher of 18 products including 5 year best seller "Homeschool Daily Planner for Curriculum" and her newest book, "Exploding Into Successful Entrepreneurship." Ann has home schooled her 6 children , two of which are CEO's of their own businesses for 15+ years. Ann has conducted hundreds of motivational workshops and has been requested to speak in 7 different states on various life enrichment topics. She has been actively teaching Empowerment Workshops to women and men, Veteran's, numerous business employees and other organizations. Ann has been featured on Nashville Fox 17 news, Renee Bobb talk radio, Devin O'Day talk radio, in the Tennessean, Leaf Chronicle, DNJ, Shelbyville Times Gazette (where she was a weekly columnist in 2011), Illinois Alliant, Upside of Money

"Faith & Finance", and The Nashville Examiner (where she is currently a weekly columnist.

CLASSES OFFERED:

FINANCIAL PLANNING—

4

"Changing Your Life Through Couponing"-A 5 part, 5 hour PowerPoint teaching series. This is a course in creating a positive financial balance within the home using every day resources. Each participant receives a copy of the corresponding 67 page workbook/review guide. See enclosed brochure.

SESSION 1- POLICY & PROCEDURE

> *Manufacturer/Retailer/Consumer Relationship
> *Deals That Deliver Dynamic Savings
> *Stacking For Super Savings

SESSION 2- COUPON SOURCES

> *Sources Without The Internet
> *Safe Sites For Ultimate Savings
> *Smart Phone Apps That Build Savings

SESSION 3-ORGANIZING & STOCKPILING

> *Clipping Without Clutter
> *Steps To Building A Balanced Stockpile
> *Preparing, Planning & Conquering

SESSION 4-DRUG STORE DEALING

> *Making Sense of Reward Programs
> *Turning Needs Into Freebies
> *Rolling Rewards For Minimal Costs

SESSION 5-COUPONING TO CHANGE YOUR LIFE

> *Reducing Debt Through Couponing
> *Building & Supporting Food Banks
> *Summing It All Up

BUSINESS MANAGEMENT—

"4 Key Steps to Becoming A Successful Entrepreneur"-This course is a 2 hour PowerPoint presentation. Each participant receives a copy of Ann's corresponding workbook entitled "Exploding Into Successful Entrepreneurship." The workbook is information packed and includes business templates for letters, promotional packets and presentations. This course will detail business building from idea to implementation. Detail will be given on marketing strategies that will enhance the success of any business. A good foundation will be instilled through Ann's personal testimony and examples of past and present entrepreneurs. The following outlines this presentation.

I. Considering Your Business

 A. Discovering Your Gift (Believing is Key to Achieving)

    1) Hobby

    2) Talent:

    3) Need:

    4) Irritation

II. Plan of Action

   A. Defeating the Opposition

    1) Past financial struggles

    2) Impatience

    3) Negative Thinking

    4) Comparison to Others

    5) Human Reasoning

    6) Unsupportive People

   B. Build A Business Plan

    1) Target Market

4

2) Sales & Marketing Potential

3) Marketing Strategy

4) Pricing

5) Distribution

6) Competition Analysis

7) Product Development

8) Cash Flow

C. Mentorship

1) Career Coaches

2) Business Owners

3) Successful Entrepreneurs

III. Expanding Your Business While Employed

A. Time Management

B. Field Mentorship

C. Home Management

D. Delegating Business Duties

IV. Investing In Your Business

A. Building a Demand

1) Test Marketing

2) Blogging & Microblogging

3) Social Networks

4) Article Distribution

5) Video Marketing

6) Press Releases

7) Vendor Fairs and Expos

B. Product/Service Submission

1) Independent Local Business'

2) Online Retailers

WORKSHOP REQUIREMENTS:

Organization must have minimum attendance of 20 people and purchase a corresponding workbook for each participant.

Workbook donation fees for each workshop are $15 per book.

In addition to the workbook, Ann's speaking donation fee for each presentation is $25 per person and may be paid by the organization or by the individuals taking the course.

Organization will be responsible for signing up attendees and providing any refreshments if desired. An online link will need to be put on the organizations website for sign up opportunities. Advertising will need to be conducted to promote this event by the organization. However, Ann Haney will advertise this event through her website www.annhaney.com as well as email list and other social media sites.

WORKSHOP SCHEDULING:

Financial Planning class may be scheduled as a 1 or 2 day event. Workshop can be customized to meet the needs of the organization. For other arrangements contact Ann. Business Management class may be scheduled on any day as an opening is available.

CONTACT:
Email-me@myownboss.com
Phone –000-000-0000
Website- annhaney.com

Ann Haney Ministries is a 501 (c) (3) organization

SAMPLE DEALER TERMS & CONDITIONS COMPONENTS

PURPOSE—— To provide potential customers with all necessary ordering information pertaining to your company's guidelines.

Part 1—Business Logo, Name of Business, Title of Form

Part 2—Shipping information

Part 3—Backorder policy and late payment guidelines

Part 4—Policy regarding damages due to shipping

Part 5—Tax Exempt Purchases

Part 6—Placing a purchase order

Part 7—How to transmit orders

Part 8—Contact information

Part 9—Product list. Include Title, Item ISBN #, Wholesale Cost and Retail

AARON PUBLISHING DEALER TERMS

1

2 Orders will be shipped UPS and shipping will be charged on the invoice that follows shipment unless you provide a UPS account #. All orders will generally be shipped within 7 business days.

3 In case of back ordered items, you will be notified via email. First order must be prepaid. All future orders due in 30 days. Late payments will be subject to a 1% monthly late fee. NO EXCEPTIONS!

4 Only products damaged during shipping can be returned for credit. Must notify immediately of any damages occurring during shipping.

5 Tax exempt # must be on file to receive exemption of taxes.

6 Please include item #, quantity, and purchase order number when placing an order.

7 Orders may be phoned in at 000-000-0000, mailed to Aaron Publishing 000 Sample Lane, Template, MS 34844 or emailed to info@aaronpublishing.com.

8 Contact us for additional information by phone, mail, or e-mail at info@aaronpublishing.com

PRODUCT LIST:

9 Products may be viewed at www.aaronpublishing.com.

TITLE	ITEM #	WHOLESALE	RETAIL
The Homeschool Daily Planner for Unit Studies	#0000	$0.00	$0.00
The Homeschool Daily Planner for High School	#0000	$0.00	$0.00
The Homeschool Daily Planner for Curriculum	#0000	$0.00	$0.00
Student Log Book And Daily Record Keeping	#0000	$0.00	$0.00

SAMPLE CONSIGNMENT COMPONENTS

PURPOSE—— This form serves as a delivery form to businesses you choose to offer your product for on a consignment basis to determine the demand for it over a period of time.

Part 1—Business Logo, Name of Business, Title of Form

Part 2—Title or Product description you are consigning

Part 3—Consignment terms in relation to length of time and payment guidelines

Part 4—Payment mailing information

Part 5—Customer cost and suggested retail

Part 6—Your signature

Part 7—Receiver's signature (all deliveries should be signed for)

Part 8—Date of delivery

SAMPLE CONSIGNMENT CONTRACT

1

JOHN DOE DESIGNERS CONSIGNMENT CONTRACT

2

"Your business Name" hereby agrees to allow _____ to put _____ copies of "Time Management For Families" Book in their store on a trial basis to determine the demand of the product.

3

At the end of 30 days from this date above mentioned store will pay *"Your Business Name"* for all copies sold. At that time it will be determined as to how many more copies will be needed. If the store determines the item to be unsuccessful all unsold copies will be returned to Ann Haney Ministries. Ann Haney Ministries reserves the right to remove copies of the above mentioned book at any time if it is determined that sales do not meet expected potential.

4

Payment should be made out to *"your business name" and* mailed to: *"your address"*

5

Customers Cost—   Retail--

6

_____

(Your Signature)

7

_____

(Store)

8

_____

(Date)

SAMPLE FACILITATOR FORM COMPONENTS

PURPOSE—— This form is necessary for anyone who schedules events with other organizations. It serves as a suggestive marketing event preparation and accountability form.

Part 1—Host Name, Email, Phone, and Location/Address/Time of Event, Date

Part 2—Checklist of items needed, marketing ideas and general guidelines

Part 3—Thank you and reinforcement of guidelines within the checklist

Part 4—Your Name and Business Name

Part 5—Cancellation Policy

Part 6—Reason for cancellation policy (this is necessary to help the host understand your commitment and work that goes into preparing for this event. Tweek this to fit your criteria.)

Part 7—Cancellation fee after 30 day grace period. (You will be sorry if you don't include this. People are more committed and take your time more seriously when this is included. I have experienced many challenges in this area and which have unfortunately resulted in this fee.)

Part 8—A final thank and looking forward to the event

Part 9—Signature of event scheduler (the one responsible for bringing you there.)

Part 10—Date of acceptance to terms of the facilitator form

Part 11—Event confirmation upon receipt of signed form (You will probably have to push to get this form returned to you. However, if a host hasn't time to go over this guideline to prepare for your arrival, they probably will not do a very good job promoting the event. Your time is your business and it must be used wisely.)

FACILITATOR FORM

HOSTING A COUPONING WORKSHOP:

Name:

Email:

Phone:

Location/Address of Event:

Date:

Time of Event:

CHECK LIST:

_____ 1. Post Flyer at event location

_____ 2. Post Event on Facebook, Twitter, at workplace, etc... (unless this is a closed event and Living In Abundance is aware of this and given okay this.

_____ 3. Make public announcement to potential attendees twice---(ex..at church, group meeting, etc...)

   _____ when event is confirmed

   _____ 1 week before event

_____ 4. Put announcement in newsletter, church bulletin, or other group producible material

_____ 5. Post event on Location Marque

------- 6. Make calls to potential group attendees

_____ 7.Gather a list of names and phone numbers of those who have showed interest in attending

_____ 8. Make follow-up calls 2 days before event to confirm their attendance.

_____ 9. If possible put in newspapers calendar of events

------10. Email Living in Abundance 2 days prior to event with an expected attendance report

------11. Email Living in Abundance with local food bank information including: name, address, drop off times, contact #, perishable/nonperishable preferences.

___12. Email Living in Abundance a copy of this form checking off the above items you will be doing to promote this event. Keep a copy for yourself to check off upon completion.

----- 13. Collect a "free will" offering at end of presentation to cover speaker's expenses. (This can be presented as----"I hope this knowledge was beneficial to you. We are going to take up a " free will offering" to help cover the speaker's expenses and be an active part in helping this ministry continue to reach others. I encourage you to support this ministry by eit14.her taking advantage of the products she offers OR making a donation in this offering."

___ 14. Yes, I have a projector for Ann's laptop to be hooked up to for the PowerPoint Presentation OR a church computer with projector Ann can put her flash drive in for the presentation.

___ 15. I need Ann to bring a projector to hook up her laptop to.

____16. Set up one 6-8 foot table in the entrance to the event for Ann's sign in and materials.

____17. Set up a small table at the front where Ann will be speaking from.

____18. Sound (Microphone) will be provided if attendance is in excess of 30 people.

Thank you for your interest in hosting this workshop. I look forward to the opportunity to serve you. I appreciate your willingness to promote this event, as it greatly helps me in planning and reaching as many people as possible with this very valuable information.

It is important you commit to doing as many of the above items as possible to insure success of this workshop for both your group as well as Living In Abundance Couponing. I am only able to continue to offer these workshops as I do with a commitment from the facilitator to help me promote them to cover the expenses involved.

Thank you again for helping me help others unlock abundance within their lives.

Ann Haney

Ann Haney Ministries —Living In Abundance Couponing

NOTE:

ANY CANCELLATIONS MUST BE MADE WITHIN 30 DAYS OF SCHEDULED EVENT(UNLESS AN EMERGENCY SITUATION OCCURS AND IS PRE-APPROVED THROUGH LIVING IN ABUNDANCE COUPONING)

 IT IS THE DESIRE OF ANN HANEY MINISTRIES TO HELP AS MANY PEOPLE AS POSSIBLE TO ACHIEVE ABUNDANCE AND MUCH TIME IS PUT INTO PREPARING TO PRESENT TO EACH COMMUNITY THROUGH PERSONALLY SPEAKING WITH EACH LOCAL STORE REGARDING THEIR RELATIONSHIP WITH THE COUPONER AND EXPECTATIONS OF, AS WELL AS HANDOUTS FOR EACH SPECIFIC AREA WHICH ARE COPIED AND PREPARED AND TRAVEL ARRANGEMENTS THAT ARE MADE IN ADVANCE. LOCAL ADVERTISING IS ALSO DONE ON THE PART OF LIVING IN ABUNDANCE COUPONING.

IT IS IMPORTANT TO REMEMBER ONCE A DATE IS CONFIRMED THIS DATE WILL NOT BE GIVEN TO SOMEONE ELSE. IT IS THE GOAL OF ANN HANEY MINISTRIES TO BE COMMITTED TO SERVING THE GROUP, ORGANIZATION, OR CHURCH TO THE FULL EXTENT OF THEIR ABILITY TO HELP THEM ACHIEVE A SOLID AND WELL PRESENTED WORKSHOP.

THE FINANCIAL SUPPORT OF THIS MINISTRY IS PROVIDED BY WORKSHOPS LIKE YOURS THROUGH PARTICIPANTS PURCHASING PRODUCTS. THIS IS THE ONLY WAY I CAN CONTINUE TO OFFER THEM FOR FREE AND TRAVEL TO MY NEXT WORKSHOP.

SAMPLE FACILITATOR FORM FOR EVENTS CONT,,,,,

7   DUE TO THE ABOVE REASONS AND THE CANCELLATIONS THAT OCCUR AFTER THE 30 DAY AL-LOTMENT OF THE SCHEDULED WORKSHOP, CANCELLATION FEES WILL BE $100.

8   THANK YOU FOR YOUR COMMITTMENT IN ADVANCE AS WE JOIN TOGETHER TO MAKE A DIF-FERENCE.

9   _____

(Signature of Organization Host/Representative)

10   _____

(Date)

11   ****Note: Event is not confirmed until this signed form is received.**

SAMPLE SIGN IN/EMAIL LIST COMPONENTS

PURPOSE—— Allows you to obtain an accurate count of attendees and compile an email list for marketing to stay connected to the attendees.

Have attendees sign in even if they do not wish to receive emails. Any of the information may be left blank or changed to create specific criteria to meet your businesses individual needs.

SAMPLE ATTENDEE SURVEY SHEET COMPONENTS

PURPOSE—— This serves as a grade report for the speaker in order to help them prepare future presentations to meet the needs of the attendees. It can advise them in areas that require improvement, give them tips and keep them motivated through positive feedback.

Part 1—Title of the presentation

Part 2— First name and last initial. This allows the person to remain pretty much anonymous.

Part 3—Positive feedback

Part 4—Areas that might need improvement

Part 5—Opportunity for the attendee to rate the handouts, workbook, or teaching aids provided with your presentation

Part 6—Time proficiency of the presentation. Was it too long, too short, or just right for the amount of material presented.

Part 7—Overall analysis of your presentation which will help you to adjust your presentation accordingly.

Part 8—This is the attendees permission to use their comments in your future materials to promote your presentations. These will often serve as great recommendations. Remember when using these use the first name, last initial, city and state. The relevancy of using the city/state is too choose from different areas to prove your creditability in a broad geographical area.

Part 9—Be sure and thank your attendees for their participation and taking the time to attend your event.

SAMPLE SIGN IN/EMAIL LIST

SIGN IN SHEET

NAME   ADDRESS   PHONE   EMAIL

CHANGING YOUR LIFE THROUGH COUPONING ATTENDEE SURVEY

First Name/ Last Initial_____

City/State _____

What was your favorite part of this teaching series?

_____

_____

What part could you use more information on?

_____

_____

What are your thoughts on the workbook supplement/handouts/teaching aids provided with this teaching?

_____

_____

Was the material presented in a timely manner?

_____

Please tell us your opinion on this presentation as a whole...

_____

_____

_____

May we use your comments as a testimony on future materials?

YES   NO

Thank you for taking time to fill out this survey and for attending this event. Your feedback is important and allows us to improve these presentations and meet the needs of the attendees.

SAMPLE BUSINESS CARD COMPONENTS

PURPOSE—— Promotes what you do. Gives people your contact information and gives your business a professional appearance. Business cards should be one of your first investments for your business.

Part 1—Logo, Name of Business, Slogan

Part 2—Website should be located on card

Part 3—Your name and position in company

Part 4—Address and phone number

Part 5—Your email

SAMPLE BUSINESS CARD

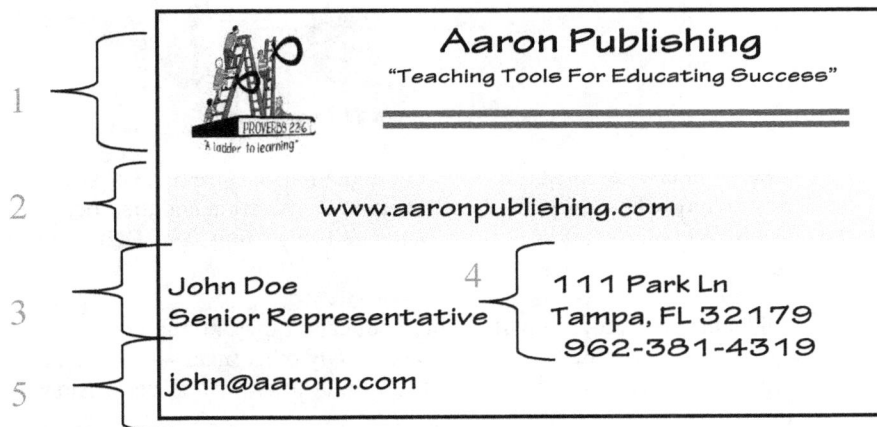

SAMPLE CHARITABLE DONATION LOG COMPONENTS

PURPOSE—— Some organizations receive donations. It is important to keep track of these donations and provide a receipt to the donor. Especially at events it is often difficult to keep track of donations without a log.

Be sure and include name, address (for mailing receipt), phone, amount, date and a place to check off when a receipt is given.

SAMPLE COPYRIGHT PAGE FOR A BOOK COMPONENTS

PURPOSE— A copyright page is crucial in the front of the book. This protects your work and lets others know your work is protected.

Part 1—Copyright date and your business
Part 2—Logo
Part 3—Email address
Part 4—Credits for content repetitively used
Part 5—Copyrighted information
Part 6—Location of printing
Part 7—You need to tell what printing material is. This allows for corrections to be made on future printings.
Part 8—A printed book usually needs an ISBN # especially if it is going to be marketed in stores. These may be obtained at www.bowker.com
Part 9— Publisher and address

1

Copyright © 2012
Ann Haney Ministries

2

3

www.annhaney.com

4

Unless otherwise noted, all Scripture quotations are from KJV/AMP Bible Parallel Edition . Copyright © 1995 by the Zondervan Corporation and the Lockman Foundation; All rights reserved, Women of Faith Message Bible. Copyright © 2008 by Women of Faith, Inc.

5

All rights reserved. No part of this publication may be reproduced, stored in a retrieval system, or transmitted, in any form or by any other means—electronic, mechanical, photocopying, recording, or otherwise—without prior written permission of Aaron Publishing.

6

Printed in the United States of America

7

First Printing, March 2012

8

ISBN 0-0000000-0-0

9

Published by
Samples Publishing
000 Front St.
Sample, IN 37194

CHARITABLE DONATION LOG

DONOR'S HOME	ADDRESS	PHONE	AMOUNT	DATE	X

SAMPLE PRESS RELEASE COMPONENTS

PURPOSE—— a professional announcement of your creditability from a news style distribution report placed on the internet. This is a report released by you to the public.

Part 1—Title of you event, product, announcement, etc..
Part 2—Writer and date
Part 3—Attention getting opening statement
Part 4—Now you have their attention, what are your offering?
Part 5— Short biography of experience
Part 6—Testimonies to give you creditability
Part 7—How can it help the reader
Part 8—Who needs what you offer?
Part 9—Extra detail
Part 10—Where can it be found?
Part 11—Website
Part 12— "I need what your offering," closing statement.
Part 13—Tags ending article
Part 14—Closing slogan for business

SAMPLE PRESS RELEASE

1 PR Log - Global Press Release Distri-   bution
Entrepreneur's Financial Empowerment Presentation

2 *By Ann Haney Ministries*
   Dated: Apr 07, 2012

3 *Tired of financial struggles due to limited job markets? Ready to break the "always employee never employer" mindset? Isn't it time you learn how to change your future & secure the future of your children in spite of the failing economy? See how.....*

4 Announcing the launch of "4 Key Steps To Successful Entrepreneurship & Raising Entrepreneurial Children." This presentation will be brought to the Self Reliance Expo in Colorado Springs, CO by motivational speaker Ann Haney. Ann will be speaking on May 18 & 19. This presentation is sure to empower you with time tested techniques through personal experience by author, publisher and homeschool mother of 6, Ann Haney. Ann is an accomplished, entertaining, professional speaker who motivates her audience to rise above their circumstances and turn hope into action. She has 3 entrepreneurial children and continues to train her other three toward self-sufficiency.

5 Ann is the author of the newly released, "Exploding Into Successful Entrepreneurship--Bringing Your God-Given Gift To The Surface For Success." When Ann was asked, "What do you hope people will learn from your book?," she replied, "I want people to stop hoping for change and unleash the power inside them to experience change."

6 What are others saying about Ann's book?

   "After reading the first chapter of your book, I know what I want to do with my life!"
   Mary B. (age 64)

   "I am thoroughly enjoying your book! It is as if you wrote the book for me! I really needed your book as a manual to get me through all of the highs and lows of entrepreneurship! Especially thank you for all of the scripture you quoted. I am already a stronger person in my faith concerning our future success because of not only the tips and encouragement in your writings, but most of all the relevant scripture you included."
   Katie K. (age 24)

7   PR What will you learn from attending this event?

* Positioning yourself to prepare for success
*Discovering your gift for success
*Defeating the opposition
*Marketing techniques
*Lessons from past and present entrepreneurs
*Building a business plan
*And much more.....

8   Who should attend this event?

*Anyone who is ready to take control of their future and discover their God-given resources to success.
*Anyone who wants to help their children prepare for a prosperous future despite the economy.
*Anyone who needs to discover the path from employee to entrepreneur
*Anyone starting a business
*Anyone needing to grow their business
*EVERYONE!!!!!

9   Ann offers some great tools in preparation for this event. Available at the expo will be a spiral bound Financial Empowerment Workbook/Study Guide--Exploding Into Successful Entrepreneurship, that corresponds with her presentation. Each workbook is filled with business templates, illustrations and motivational instructions to empower the future entrepreneur. Also available is her new 164 page book--Exploding Into Successful Entrepreneurship that will inspire you to jump into action and use the tools found in the corresponding workbook/study guide. These two books provide a complete educational course for the student or adult who desires to start their own business or just discover their God-given gift!

10   Event: Self Reliance Expo
Date: May 18-19
Time: 10am-7pm, 9am-7pm
Location:Freedom Financial Services Center
3650 N.Nevada Ave
Colorado Springs, CO 80907

11   For more information on this life changing event contact.......
http://www.selfrelianceexpo.com/

Learn More About Ann........
http://www.annhaney.com/

12   Come see what everyone is talking about and why Ann has been asked to speak so many places across the United States!

13   ###

14   Ann Haney Ministries is dedicated to helping men, women and children discover their God-given abilities and unleash them to produce abundant living.

FREE LANCE WRITING CONTRACT COMPONENTS

PURPOSE-— Serves as an agreement between a writer whose work will be published in a companies periodical or used on the internet. This serves to protect the rights of the writer and the publisher.

Part 1— Two parties the agreement is between

Part 2—The contract should have a beginning date and information regarding the type of content each article will have. In other words if you are writing on financial empowerment it might say something like, "Articles will contain information related to finances in some manner."

Part 3—Payment agreements must be made prior to the job beginning. It should include: how much and when payment is expected.

Part 4—Rights as agreed to regarding rights given to the publication. This secures the rights of the writer as sole ownership of their material.

Part 5—Dissolution of agreement. This allows either party the ability to dissolve this contract. It is a good idea to have this in writing with a specified amount of time.

Part 6— Publication should date and sign as well as the writer.

VIDEO SCRIPT FOR PRODUCT/EVENT PROMOTION COMPONENTS

PURPOSE— This allows the viewing audience to connect with you personally. They will know what to expect when they arrive at the event by hearing how passionate you are about your topic. If you are promoting a product your expressions and excitement will become contagious to your audience and entice them into participation.

Part 1—Introduce yourself and your product to your viewing audience.

Part 2—Testimonials are a plus. If they can't make an appearance use text in the video to emphasize

Part 3—Invite them to become an active part of what you're promoting. Give them information to further their learning by sending them to your website/event etc...

SAMPLE VIDEO SCRIPT FOR PRODUCT/EVENT

1   "Hi, my name is John Doe and I have discovered a quick, easy and effective way to prepare your pool for the summer. One application of Single Shock will turn your pool crystal clear in 24 hours.

2   Here's what people are saying about Single Shock:

"Single Shock is easy to use and produced results that astonished me."
Terry S.

"The results I received from Single Shock would have cost me hundred's of dollars with other products. I saved money and time."
Kim P.

3   Come see for yourself how Single Shock can save "your pool and your money" at the Annual Summer and Swim Expo, Sat. May 23 at Cartright Convention Center in Nashville, TN. Visit us at sparkleshock.com to find out all the details and register for a $25 summer supply.

SAMPLE FREE LANCE WRITING CONTRACT

STANDARD FREELANCE WRITING PUBLICATION AGREEMENT

This agreement is between _____ and _____

                                (writer)   (publication)

Assignment:

As of _____ it was decided upon that the above mentioned writer would write articles for
    (date)
the above mentioned publication. The articles will be _____ related content. It is understood upon accepting this agreement that the above mentioned writer does use related principles in the articles for life application purposes.

A payment of _____per each article will be paid to the above writer on a monthly basis. This fee
    ($ amount)
is to be paid weekly as agreed upon between the writer and publication.

Each article remains sole ownership of the writer mentioned above. The publication above is given " One-Time Rights" (granting publication the non-exclusive right to use material once) by _____ to publish each article. Each article may remain on the internet website
    (writer)
for the publication a total of 1 year from its original appearance.

Either party may void this contract with a thirty day notice given upon written notification.

_____
    (Date)

_____
    (writer)

_____
    (Publication)

93

PUBLIC SERVICE ANNOUNCEMENT (PSA) COMPONENTS

PURPOSE-— To advertise something of interest to the public in the commercial advertising sector of media or radio. These can serve as a great way to familiarize the public with your event. (Usually these serve as a tool for non profit organizations.) A PSA must prove to be a broadcast in the public interest.

Tips for a PSA—

Find out length of advertising (It might be a good idea to do several 10, 15, 20, 30 second PSA's)
Written format required (typed-double or triple spaced)
Email, Fax or via Mail, Video or Recording
Deadline of Submission

(All of these things can be found out on their website or by contacting public affairs director of the station)

Part 1— When: will tell the station when the PSA should air. This might be "specific date", "till further notice" or "immediate." **Time:** length of below PSA. **Organization:** What organization is presenting the PSA. **Title:** What the event is called
Part 2—Hook the listeners with an attention getting opening. Often a question will get them thinking. Follow with the answer to what they need. Give them enough information to convince them they can attend (location, time, etc..) but keep them inquiring after the PSA is over by giving them your website/phone number. A closing statement to reinforce the opening one can drive them to discovering more about the event.
Part 3—These tags are used to show ending in a release to the media.

SAMPLE PUBLIC SERVICE ANNOUNCEMENT

PUBLIC SERVICE ANNOUNCEMENT (PSA)

1
When—IMMEDIATE
Time— 30 second
Organization—Fairfield Fitness Center
Title—Fitness For All

2
Are you looking for a way to include fitness into your busy schedule? If this is you, come celebrate Fitness For All this Tuesday morning at 9:00 AM June 8 at the Annual Fitness Fair. This event will take place at the Fairfield Fitness Facility in Fairhaven, TN. Visit fairfieldfitness.org or call 888-888-8888 and find out how you can be fit and flexible with your busy schedule!

3
###

BROCHURE/FLYER PROMOTIONAL COMPONENTS

PURPOSE—— To advertise your business/product by getting something in the hands of potential customers. People in general are fast paced, tell me quick consumers. When you put something in their hands to read at their leisure you will often discover come back customers.

Brochures and Flyers can be great ways to market your business/product. There are many types, however the components are generally the same even though the size and format may vary.

Tips for designing brochures and flyers—

1. The product/service/business must grasp the readers attention without them having to search for who you are or what you offer.
2. A "hook them" statement or question needs to follow to entice them to read on. If they get bored here, nothing else you say will have much effect.
3. Graphics should be clear, relative to content, consistent in theme, and NOT overused.
4. Colors should compliment each other and not draw away from the written content.
5. Purpose, Benefits and Belief should be clearly brought to the reader's attention.
6. Contact information should be easily identifiable to the reader. If they can't find you they probably won't have confidence in your ability to meet their need.

Specifics for flyers:

1. Business name and logo
2. "Hook them" statement (depending on size of flyer)
3. Specialties offered
4. Confidence building statement (ex. "Keeping Customers Satisfied for Over 20 years")
5. Contact information

Specifics for brochures:

1. Business name and logo
2. "Hook them" statement on first page to encourage further reading
3. Mission Statement
4. Products/Services Offered
5. Experience
6. Testimonials
7. Business Background (how long in business, etc..)
8. Customer Guarantee

BUSINESS PLAN COVER LETTER COMPONENTS

PURPOSE—— **Serves as the cover letter to your business plan which will follow on the next pages.**

Part 1— Business Logo
Part 2—Business name and slogan
Part 3—Title of document
Part 4—Copyright year of document
Part 5—Month and year of preparation
Part 6—Owner's name, address, phone and email

BUSINESS PLAN COMPONENTS

(These will also serve as the parts for the table of contents)

Part 1—This section will be your mission statement of the beliefs that your business is built on and the vision you have for your business
Part 2—In this section you will detail the services and/or products you offer
    Marketing strategies you will use to grow your business, potential and target market
    Competition analysis will come next
    Operating procedures of business including distribution, pricing and product development
    Listing of employees and duties responsible for
    Board of Directors
    Insurance carried by the business including property, liability, health, etc..
Part 3—This section will include the financial structure of the business including: sales potential, loans, equipment and supplies owned, profit and loss statements, long term analysis of the business and cash flow
Part 4—Legal documents should be included with your business plan. These will include: tax returns, lease agreements, supplier contracts and licenses.

1

2

ANN HANEY MINISTRIES

Helping People Unlock Abundant Futures

3

BUSINESS PLAN

4

Copyright©2012

5

May 2012

6

**Ann Haney
00 Front St.
Sample, IN 00000
000-000-0000
me@myownboss.com**

SAMPLE BUSINESS PLAN TABLE OF CONTENTS

1 {

   I. Summary
        A. Mission Statement
        B. Vision

2 {

   II. Business Detail
        A. Services
        B. Products
        C. Marketing
            1. Strategies
            2. Potential
            3. Target Market
        D. Competition
        E. Operating
            1. Distribution
            2. Pricing
            3. Product Development
        F. Fund Raising Plan
        G. Employees
        H. Board of Directors
            1. Board Policies

3 {

   III. Financial Detail
        A. Start Up Expenses
        B. Operating Costs
        C Long Term Analysis (3 year)

4 {

   IV. Legal Documents
        A. Tax Returns
        B. Lease Agreements
        C. Supplier Contracts
        D. Licenses

SAMPLE BUSINESS PLAN

I. SUMMARY

AHM is dedicated to helping people unlock abundant futures by motivating them to use tools and resources available in everyday life. It is the goal of this ministry to equip people with motivation that moves them to action changing their circumstances for the better. AHM connects people with achiever mindsets by helping them discover their God-given abilities and surface them for success.

A. MISSION STATEMENT

Helping people who find themselves victims of circumstances by training them to be overcoming achievers who unlock abundant futures.

B. VISION

*Restructuring the way people think
* Providing resources for success
* Equipping entrepreneurs
* Helping people grow from idea to increase

II. BUSINESS DETAIL

AHM is in business to offer ministry services and donation based product tools to help people achieve their greatest potential.

A. SERVICES

AHM offers extensive services based upon the individual needs of the individual. Evaluation of the individuals needs are determined and services are performed to provide the greatest potential success for the individual.

* Power Point Presentations
* Phone Counseling
* Email Counseling
* Multi Level Training Classes
* Instructional Manual Classes
*Interactive Training Classes

B. PRODUCTS

We offer a wide variety of products to support the function of this ministry/business. All products are on a set donation basis and used to help support the continuing functions of this ministry.

*Coupon Organizational Tools (binder/pouches/coupon holders/dividers)
* Handbooks
* Videos
* Audios
* Mini books

99

C. MARKETING

Several marketing strategies are used to reach as many people as possible with these life changing strategies.

1. STRATEGIES

* You Tube/Press Releases/PSA's/Twitter/LinkedIn
* Motivational Presentations That Equip People to Strive For Their Full Potential.
*Flyers, Brochures and Promotional DVD's

2. POTENTIAL

The potential of these strategies has the ability to enable more people to become self employed free lance individuals who will work their own schedules while setting their own income potential and changing their standard of living.

3. TARGET MARKET

Target Market of this ministry is to reach those who are starting a career, limited in a current career and change the financial status of the elderly who need to increase their income potential.

* High School Graduates
* Underpaid Employees
* Social Security Recipients

D. COMPETTION

The competition to this ministry is limited and only enhances the furtherance of this ministry by networking together to join efforts in creating a common goal—changing the economy of people for future stability.

E. OPERATIONS

The operations of this ministry includes distribution of products with minimal donation fees for designed educational and motivational resources. These resources are designed as tools that reinforce the mindset of the overcomer and challenge the struggling entrepreneur to achieve the success they set out to obtain.

1. DISTRIBUTION

Distribution area includes but is not limited to online retailers, locally owned book stores, individual sales and website sales within the United States. Also, these products are offered at all speaking engagements to help reinforce the presentation and develop life application mindsets within the participants.

2. PRICING

This is not applicable due to the organization being a non profit organization. All pricing is donation based according to the guidelines set forth by the 501 (c) (3) non profit organizations government guidelines.

3. PRODUCT DEVELOPMENT

Products will continually be developed based on arising needs of individuals to bring betterment to their overall financial strategies and situations. Products are designed in house by the graphics design staff and founder.

F. FUNDRAISING PLAN

Sponsorship will be sought from various businesses to further this ministry. Drawings will be held at events for items donated by these businesses. These items may include but are not limited to books, gift cards, DVD's, CD's, etc... Each sponsored event will require preregistration and the completion of a facilitator form by the host of the event.

G. EMPLOYEES

AHM is currently operated by a small staff including presenter, event coordinator, secretary, graphics designer and videographer. All employees are currently on a voluntary basis. As the demands of this ministry grow and the need for extended hours is required the staff will be put on a salary based around the duties assigned.

H. BOARD OF DIRECTORS

Chair—
Vice Chair—
Secretary—
Bookkeeper—
Support—

1. BOARD POLICIES

*Any uprising concerns within the administration or functionality of Ann Haney Ministry will result in a meeting of the board members to make decisions based upon the best interest of the organization.

*All donations to the ministry will be recorded and distributed accordingly with the approval of the chair and vice chair in agreement.

*A monthly meeting will be conducted and minutes taken to discuss the old and new business of the ministry in order to keep ongoing communication and furtherance of the ministry.

III. FINANCIAL DETAIL

The income in this ministry is designated to meet the expenses required to run this ministry as well as provide the charitable needs of specific individuals and organizations.

A. START UP EXPENSES

* Automobile (gas/insurance)—
*Equipment (computer/copier/duplicator/CD printer/binder)—
*Office Supplies (paper/DVD's/CD's/ink/product)—
*Website (creation/hosting)—
*Marketing (flyers/brochures/business cards/banners/ posters)—
*Accounting —
Total—

B. OPERATING COSTS

*Automobile (gas/insurance)—
*Equipment (electricity/service maintenance)
*Office Supplies (paper/DVD's/CD's/ink/product reorder)—
*Website (hosting)—
*Marketing (flyers/brochures/business cards)—
*Accounting —

C. LONG TERM ANALYSIS (3 YEAR PLAN)

It is the expectation of this ministry to grow the marketing area nationwide which will increase the financial needs as well as provide more opportunity for jobs. With this growth it is the goal of Ann Haney Ministries to not only reach others with life changing information but to support the charities that make a difference in the following areas:

*Veteran's
*Human Trafficking
*Orphan's
*Homeless
*Abused Women

IV. LEGAL DOCUMENTS

(Will be attached here)

NOTES

RESOURCES

_____

_____

_____

_____

_____

_____

_____

_____

_____

_____

_____

_____

_____

Financial Empowerment Course Completion Certificate

For
"Exploding Into Successful Entrepreneurship"

This certifies that _____ has successfully completed all the requirements of this course of study detailed in the Financial Empowerment Workbook and read "Exploding Into Successful Entrepreneurship" by Ann Haney.

And is entitled to this certificate

This _____ day of _____ 20 _____

_____
(instructor-if applicable)

_____
(student)

For More Great Products

From

Ann Haney Ministries

Visit Us At

www.annhaney.com

www.ingramcontent.com/pod-product-compliance
Lightning Source LLC
Chambersburg PA
CBHW051226200326
41519CB00025B/7259